GOOD MORNING,
LORD

Everyday Prayers for Everyday People

JOSEPH T. SULLIVAN

TWENTY-THIRD PUBLICATIONS
Mystic, Connecticut 06355

Nihil obstat
Michel J. St. Pierre
Censor Librorum

Imprimatur
Most Reverend Kenneth A. Angell
Bishop of Burlington
July 14, 1994

Twenty-Third Publications
185 Willow Street
P.O. Box 180
Mystic, CT 06355
(203) 536-2611
800-321-0411

ISBN 0-89622-593-3
Library of Congress Catalog Card Number 93-61502
Printed in the U.S.A.

"Some time ago, when Father Sullivan was the Communications Director of the Diocese of Burlington, he came to me with the idea of adding a morning prayer to our station's official sign-on. It seemed a wonderful idea and was begun almost immediately. It is still a part of WCAX-TV's daily sign-on. Many viewers over the years have written to thank us for 'Good Morning, Lord' and say they look forward to each day's prayer.

"I'm sure that the readers of *Good Morning, Lord* will enjoy these prayers as much as our viewers have for almost two decades."

Ken Greene
Director, Public Affairs
WCAX-TV, Burlington, Vermont

"For some 15 years, Fr. Joseph Sullivan woke up Vermont's faithful with 'Good Morning, Lord' and a prayer. At least a dozen radio stations and two television channels used the 'Good Morning, Lord' series when they signed on each day. Reading this book was like glimpsing into a diary of the good years I worked with Fr. Sullivan, with each prayer reminiscent of a page out of his life, complete with fears, foibles, joys, and hopes. And Fr. Sullivan shared these intimacies willingly, as though conversing with a favorite friend, for indeed he was.

"Fr. 'Sulli-vision' as fans called him, never tired of writing, voicing, and producing 'Good Morning, Lord.' As he says in the final prayer of this collection: 'What is more simple than loving and wanting to communicate with the one you love?'"

Gloria J. Gibson
Communications Director
Diocese of Burlington

"*Good Morning, Lord: Everyday Prayers for Everyday People* is a pure ray of love aimed straight and true at the heart of God. It ranges from simple acts of self-giving: 'Good morning, Lord; thank you for the new day, which is yours not mine...' to poetic passages: 'We walk through the day unaware of the blessings around us; sharpen our powers of observation, Lord, to be aware of the poor, the lonely, the sensitive.' Fr. Joseph T. Sullivan brings a sweetness of spirit to his work that freshens his many prayers with joy."

Fr. John Catoir
Director, The Christophers

Contents

GOOD MORNING,
LORD

Invitation

How accessible is God? Always present, God is only a prayer away.

Good Morning, Lord provides prayers for everyone, one for each day of the year. They speak to God in everyday language, expressing the concerns, hopes, disappointments, sorrows, needs, joys of everyday people like you.

Your relationship with God develops through dialogue, through listening. In prayer you converse with the most lovable and most loving God. In prayer you are in contact with Someone who loves you individually, personally, with an overwhelming love.

Say "Good evening, Lord" instead of "Good morning, Lord" if the day has flown. Should a prayer especially appeal to you, pray it often, regardless of the day; reflect on it, line by line, savoring it. If another should not appeal to you, pass it over and let your heart speak—or listen—spontaneously to God. In either event, pray daily and pray often.

Divine Presence

Good morning, Lord.
Please be with me today, at my side,
    guiding me, inspiring me.
As I get all tied up in the day's agenda,
    wrapped up in the important matters of life,
    I know nothing escapes your loving concern.
I am constantly in your presence.
I may find it difficult
    to recall a week from now
    what is so important today,
    but may I never forget that I do not walk alone.
Help me to be conscious
    of your loving presence. Amen.

"Hello" and "Goodnight"

Good morning, Lord.
It's easy to think of you at the start of a new day.
But as the day wears on,
    I have to be mindful
    that prayer isn't only for mornings or evenings.
Prayer is communication, conversation with you;
    the lines are always open,
    even when there are no words on them.
Saying "hello" when the sun rises
    and "goodnight" when it sets
    scarcely nourishes our relationship.
You are an integral part of my life,
    the giver of life itself, and my destiny.
Help me to be in touch with you during the day,
    even for a brief moment. Amen.

January 3
Happy Opportunity
Good morning, Lord.
Let me help to make someone happy today.
Once in a while, someone surprises me
    with a thoughtful gesture or word.
They go out of their way with a personal touch.
The gesture touches my human spirit like magic.
I think, "Hey, you've made my day."
I'd like to do that to another,
    to bring a smile to the face of another.
Maybe I'll just phone someone and compliment her.
Perhaps I'll tell the diner cook he makes good coffee.
The grace to be thoughtful of others, Lord;
    that's what I need,
    and that's what the world needs. Amen.

January 4
Forgiving
Good morning, Lord.
Let me maintain a forgiving attitude today.
Not that I'm expecting trouble.
There's no intention of being condescending,
    but it's par for the course—
    simply being realistic—
    that someone may annoy me
    or even harm me today.
It may not even be on purpose.
So in advance, anticipating the possible,
    let me try to be good-natured and forgiving.
Forgive us our trespasses
    as we forgive others.
Grace me with a forgiving heart. Amen.

In Pursuit of Happiness

Good morning, Lord.

It's another day and I'm still in pursuit of happiness.

I search for happiness from hour to hour

    in people's smiles,

    in praise for work well done,

    in my possessions,

    in encouragement when the going gets tough.

My interest in big money gaming,

    the lottery, the give-away shows

    suggests I may identify happiness with money.

How does that Sermon on the Mount go?

It's echoing through the centuries:

    "Blessed are the poor in spirit."

I'm looking for happiness, Lord;

    teach me where it really lies. Amen.

Quiet Communication

Good morning, Lord.

If I am very quiet and still,

    will you speak to my heart?

Peace and quiet seem to be the acceptable setting

    for prayer, for conversation with you.

Let me not be in a hurry,

    anxious for the time to pass.

May my room just now be a chapel for a few minutes.

I invite you in for a visit.

I promise to listen, to be receptive,

    to psych myself into the most ideal disposition.

How may I please you this day?

Speak, Lord, for your servant is listening. Amen.

January 7

New Day

Good morning, Lord.
The sun is coming up,
    roosters are crowing, alarm clocks are ringing.
It's a new day, a time to praise you,
    an opportunity to honor you by a sincere life.
This day is different than other days—
    it has never happened before.
This day has hope.
It has promise.
I pray that I may please you today—
    whatever the cost!
Lord, you are the loving God of us all.
Thank you for this new day. Amen.

January 8

Peacemaker

Good morning, Lord.
Make me an instrument of your peace today.
Let me be a peacemaker.
In the Sermon on the Mount we heard,
    "Blessed are the peacemakers;
    they shall be called the children of God."
I pray that this peace may begin with me,
    here in my own heart.
If there are any who have offended me,
    I forgive them.
If I have offended others,
    I'll try to patch things up.
Take all bitterness from my being.
I wish to be at peace
    with all my brothers and sisters. Amen.

God's Will

Good morning, Lord.
May I know your will this day?
We pray, "Thy will be done."
Your will is our direction, our guidance.
We have the scriptures,
    and we have the commandments.
These teach us your will.
Then there are those confusing situations,
    life's complications when your will
    isn't so clear to us.
What do we do here and now
    in these special circumstances?
Lord, you alone know all things.
May we know the correct road to follow. Amen.

Do You Love Me?

Good morning, Lord.
Tell me, show me, do you love me?
I'll bet that question has been asked
    a few zillion times.
How sweet it is to have someone tell us
    we are loved.
And I'm sure you love to hear it too.
People, though, sometimes question your love—
    myself included—
    especially in times of tragedy, calamity, distress.
But deep down, Lord,
    I know your love is steadfast and forever.
Let me always remember that you are love,
    and that you love us all beyond measure. Amen.

January 11

Trusting God

Good morning, Lord.
What will this day have in store for me?
Each morning starts a new adventure.
Some say it is better not to know what lies ahead;
    we don't worry about it then.
Your grace is sufficient for us.
It gives us an opportunity
    to put our hand in yours,
    to walk through life with faith,
    trusting you.
Is there any other way, really?
I can't think of anyone better to trust
    than you, our loving God. Amen.

January 12

Generosity

Good morning, Lord.
May I praise you and glorify you this day
    by a good life.
I want to do what is noble and kind,
    to accomplish deeds
    of generosity and thoughtfulness.
In my heart I feel it is possible
    to meet the personal challenge of a better life,
    to be the person you call me to be.
Let my pettiness remain in the past.
It is beneath me and so unworthy of you.
Beginning today—a fresh beginning—
    I want to be like the self-sacrificing,
    inspired heroes of today I read about.
Inspire me as well. Amen.

Never Look Back

Good morning, Lord.

Help me not to look back at my sins—
  you know how many they are!

I know that once I recognize the error,
  correct it and make amends,
  I'm supposed to move on,
  toward better and greater things.

Brooding, feeling sorry for myself, scolding myself
  are unproductive and silly.

They fail to recognize your merciful forgiveness,
  your unmistakable love for me.

Hey! What mistakes? This is a new day.

I'm on your side, Lord,
  and you're on mine. Amen.

Invitation to Ask

Good morning, Lord.

Your holy word tells us,
  "Ask and you shall receive.
  Seek and you will find.
  Knock and it will be opened."

Your words are an invitation to approach you,
  encouragement to turn to you, Lord,
  the giver of all good gifts.

Some people say they hate to ask
  because it sounds like they have the "gimmies."

Well, if I loved somebody who had needs I could fill,
  I'd feel bad if they didn't let me help.

Let me approach you with the confidence
  that should be mine as your child. Amen.

January 15
Equal Rights
Good morning, Lord.
I notice more and more
   in the news reports
   that many people's civil rights are not respected.
Men, women, children seem deprived
   of the opportunity
   and the recognition due to them.
If only we had the vision
   to see one another as you see us:
   as equals.
We are all beautiful in your sight—
   made according to your image and likeness.
Free our minds and hearts from prejudice.
Liberate us from our fears of what is different
   and from our selfishness. Amen.

January 16
Liberating Commandments
Good morning, Lord.
It appears to me there's a lot of sinning going on:
   violence, dishonesty, infidelity, sexism,
   pornography, racism, greed.
Sometimes it seems overwhelming
   how we disrespect one another,
   take advantage of one another's weaknesses.
I guess we all are subject to temptation—
   and there but for the grace of God go I.
Your commandments guide us
   in respecting one another's rights.
They liberate us, not restrict us.
Thy will be done, Lord. Amen.

My Importance

Good morning, Lord.
When I think of the billions of people like me
    in this wide, wonderful world,
    I realize how insignificant I am.
How can I really matter?
Then I recall that you love each of us individually.
Knowing that you love me makes me realize
    I am not insignificant at all.
I am very important.
Help me this day to walk worthily of the dignity
    you have bestowed upon me, your child.
Let me respect every person,
    for everyone is precious
    and important in your eyes. Amen.

Love Your Enemy

Good morning, Lord.
I'm going to pray for someone I dislike today.
No one is going to know about it,
    except you and me.
If I love only those who love me, what's that?
Even the pagans are capable
    of that kind of reciprocity.
But if I honestly try to love my "enemy,"
    do good to those who wish me ill,
    that's being magnanimous—great-souled.
I'd like to think of myself as that kind of character:
    bigger than life, generous to a fault, self-effacing.
I may not measure up to that,
    but with your help, I'll do what I can. Amen.

January 19

Appreciation

Good morning, Lord.

May I never knowingly discourage someone
by failing to show appreciation.

Help me to share the enthusiasm of a child
discovering pretty butterflies.

If someone proudly shows me a work of creation
or offers a good suggestion,
let me show my appreciation.

Inspire me to be interested in people's work,
their hobbies, skills, and virtues.

Life is so much more fulfilling when people share
their creations and their appreciation.

Thank you, Lord, for your love
and for all the encouraging words we receive—
and give—this day. Amen.

January 20

My Heart

Good morning, Lord.

I may not be fully awake yet,
but I want to speak to you
at the start of this new day.

Perhaps it really doesn't matter what I say
so long as my heart is in the right place.

Words don't always come out right in conversation,
or come out at all.

But I don't have to worry
about you, Lord, not understanding.

You read my heart.

Thank you, Lord, for this new day.

I'll try to make it a good one for you. Amen.

Morning Smile

Good morning, Lord.
I was just thinking,
  everybody starts the day
  not knowing completely what it's going to bring.
Even so, we should all start the day with a smile.
We've got you, Lord, haven't we?
You don't tell us what's ahead,
  but you assure us of your loving presence.
If we don't smile, it's our own fault.
Happy are they who start the day with a smile.
That may not be one of the original beatitudes,
  but it is a positive outlook
  that I know you will bless.
Bless us all, Lord. Amen.

Real Freedom

Good morning, Lord.
What can I do about freedom today?
Who can I liberate?
What can I do to help people remove their chains?
I read about people who are slaves
  to the bottle, to drink, to power,
  who are dependent on drugs, on nicotine,
  and on habits that tie them up and lead them
  in a direction they would rather not go.
I guess I should really start with myself, Lord,
  while I'm at it.
Who isn't hooked on something
  that's leading to no good?
It can be done with your grace. Amen.

January 23

Inspiration

Good morning, Lord.

Thank you for all the creative people in our world,
    artists of all kinds: sculptors, authors, song writers,
    painters, musicians, architects.

They can pick up our spirits
    and carry us away from the humdrum and routine;
    they can lead us to nobler thoughts.

Help them to use their talents
    for the noble, the inspiring, the uplifting.

They have such enormous capability for good;
    their collective influence is powerful.

Inspire them with your creative spirit, Lord.

Help them to show us how to look up at the stars,
    not down at the mud and the puddles. Amen.

January 24

Little Children

Good morning, Lord.

May we always see your beauty in children:
    the sweet, the unspoiled, the innocent.

Unless we become like little children,
    we cannot enter the Kingdom of God.

These words tell us how we are to preserve
    those beautiful childlike qualities.

They bring us joy.

Little boys, little girls belong to you in a special way;
    they are particularly a reflection
    of your simplicity and goodness.

They laugh and skip through life with abandon.

And that's the way I would like to be
    in my relationship with you, Lord. Amen.

14

Slowing Down

Good morning, Lord.
I think I'll slow down the merry-go-round of life today.
I couldn't stop the world if I wanted to.
Dashing about from one end of the day to the other
    is a life pattern for too many of us.
We hardly see anything or hear anything
    worth holding on to and appreciating.
We really don't stop to smell the roses.
Slowing down to observe, to reach out,
    to understand, and to care
        may just improve the quality of my life—
        and others'.
Help me to slow down and wake up
    to what really matters. Amen.

My Blessings

Good morning, Lord.
Let me savor and appreciate my blessings today:
    the food I eat, the pleasures I enjoy,
    the friends I meet,
    the family I'm part of,
    the land I live in.
It's not right to take what I have received for granted—
    and what do I have that I have not received?
It's a shame not to recognize
    the giver of the good gifts—
    and to learn about the giver from the gifts.
Everything I have, all that I enjoy,
    all are gifts from you, generous Donor.
Thank you for this day's gifts. Amen.

Refugees

Good morning, Lord.
Refugees are on my mind this morning.
I think I'm living in the age of refugees.
Thousands try to escape oppression in foreign lands,
    fleeing political and religious persecution.
They make daring efforts,
    risking persecution if they are caught,
    brave stormy seas in small boats,
    seek new homelands.
Men, women, and children look toward our land.
I can ask myself, who are my neighbors?
They are in the headlines each morning.
I pray for all refugees.
May my heart be sensitive to their plight
    and my mind alert for their relief. Amen.

January 28

Hope

Good morning, Lord.
Nothing is ever hopeless knowing you are near.
The darkest night cannot hide your saving light.
In our heavy moods we forget at times
    how much you love us,
    how truly near you are,
    even though you may feel distant.
We neglect to look up and see your light,
    to see your presence in the events of my life.
Why should we fear when you can say the word
    and things can become better?
"Let there be light" you said, and there was.
Grant me the grace of deep-seated hope. Amen.

A Good Deed

Good morning, Lord.
May I do something for someone today,
    perhaps go out of my way
    to assist someone without their asking,
    without expecting recognition or gratitude.
They say "nobody does nothing
    for nobody any more."
If it's true, what can I do—day in and day out—
    to turn that around?
Doing to others as we would have them do to us
    means reaching out generously, blindly,
    touching others' lives.
Faith without works is dead.
May I do a good deed today, maybe even two. Amen.

Reading Directions

Good morning, Lord.
How often after fumbling with the assembly
    of a toy or appliance,
    do I have to remind myself
    to read the directions carefully.
If the toy or gadget doesn't work right,
    perhaps it's not assembled correctly.
Let me carefully read your directions
    for a better world.
If society, my neighborhood, is not working smoothly,
    lovingly, perhaps it's just not put together right.
We haven't followed your directions,
    which are your commandments.
Teach us all to value your guidelines, Lord,
    your directions. Amen.

January 31
Divine Providence

Good morning, Lord.

When we are battered with snow and ice,
    when temperatures plunge
    and the wind bites relentlessly,
    we appreciate central heating and fireplaces.

For all our technological and scientific progress
    we are still at the mercy of the elements.

Are they not but a forceful reminder
    of your power, Lord,
    that some things are beyond our control
    and decision making?

I know you do not subject us
    to blizzards, sleet, and wild winds
    so that we don't forget our relationship with you—
    a loving God is not intent on making us miserable—
    but we do rely on your providence. Amen.

Time for Conversation

Good morning, Lord.
I'm starting the day on the right foot,
    praying, talking with you.
I have the time to talk.
Wouldn't it be foolish
    if I didn't have time for you?
Who do I think I am
    dashing about from sunrise to sunset
    without so much as a "Hello, Lord"?
But I remembered.
It's one of my better habits
    starting the day asking for your blessing.
Thank you for the inspiration,
    and for the brand new day. Amen.

Something to Say

Good morning, Lord.
I've got something to say this morning:
How great it is to be alive!
Are there people who have nothing to say to you,
    give you the silent treatment,
    like quarreling lovers?
I suppose there are folks who do not pray.
Well, how good it is to be able to speak with you,
    to express myself and listen to you.
I don't even have to pick up the phone;
    the rates are inexpensive, too.
Do I sound a little frivolous?
It's a great day to be alive.
Thank you. Amen.

Reaching Out

Good morning, Lord.
It's difficult to believe
    there is not enough to go around.
I simply cannot conceive of my generous God
    not providing the necessities of life.
Yet poverty exists; basic necessities are not met.
Millions go to bed hungry.
Love your neighbor as yourself—
    the great commandment—
    reminds me to reach out,
        to see if love can make the difference.
Lord, may my heart and courage be right
    to meet this challenge. Amen.

Life at All Stages

Good morning, Lord.
Sometimes when I look into the faces of the old,
I imagine how they appeared in their prime.
They are, after all, the same younger people
    only with added years.
The young, the middle-aged, the old
    together provide a perspective—
    a balanced society perhaps—
        of where we come from, where we are going.
According to St. Augustine,
    we were created for you, Lord,
    and our restlessness is stilled only with you.
May we appreciate all of human life—
    all ages, all stages—
        created in your image. Amen.

Riding Out the High Waves

Good morning, Lord.
Let this be a good day,
   a smooth one, a day without hassle.
I know every day has its challenges,
   its temptations and trials,
   its mistakes and successes.
Yet, it's not the day really that's the problem,
   just myself.
What I ask for is the grace
   to ride out the high waves and strong winds,
   the ability to keep my perspective
   while plunging into life's absorbing details
   and turbulent events.
I'll try to remember where I am, who I am,
   that Earth is Earth and heaven is heaven.
Let everyone have a good day. Amen.

Kind Words

Good morning, Lord.
"Never let evil talk pass your lips;
   say only good things people need to hear."
Encouraging words,
   the way we ought to communicate.
We have so much potential for good
   with positive thinking, positive speech.
Evil talk, the misuse of the gift of speech—
   words ill-befitting God or human beings—
   are better left unsaid.
Lord, let this be my motto today:
"Only kind words are spoken here." Amen.

February 7

Super Day

Good morning, Lord.
This is going to be a super day
   because I want it to be.
It is, as they say,
   the first day in the rest of my life.
Anxieties, fears, hang-ups can drag me down.
Life is too short to be inhibited
   by this negative way of thinking.
Lord, you have given me life
   and a wonderful world to live in.
Let me not live it, Lord,
   under a cloud of doom
   that more often than not
   I imagine or exaggerate.
The weather notwithstanding,
   I know this is going to be a super day. Amen.

February 8

Get It in Motion

Good morning, Lord.
I'd like to start my day
   with some get-up-and-go,
   to get it all in motion with a lot of drive
   as if I just came out of the locker room
   after a coach's pep talk,
   all fired up, charged for action.
That's the way I'd like it to be today, Lord,
   praising you, honoring you
   by doing something important for those I meet.
Let me know the joy of serving others.
That's the grace I pray for this morning. Amen.

Routine

Good morning, Lord.
A new day is like a clean blackboard.
I am about to write this days's events.
Some things happen beyond my control,
    but still life is what I'll make of it.
What spectaculars shall I chalk up today?
A million-dollar business deal?
First prize in a writing contest?
Winner of the tennis tournament?
Well, perhaps not for this day-dreamer!
Whatever happens, let me be considerate
    in many small, unspectacular ways.
This way, Lord, my life will be a success.
Your grace is what I need for this. Amen.

Happiness

Good morning, Lord.
When I meet happy people,
    I ask myself why I am not a happier person.
Most of the time I just keep busy
    and do not think whether I am happy or not.
Then someone asks, "Are you happy?"
I think, "This happiness business is relative."
How happy can a person be?
Some folks remain quite cheerful,
    despite poverty and other difficulties.
Others, who seems to have it all,
    moan and groan, seemingly without reason.
Knowing you, Lord, being with you
    is the key to happiness. Amen.

February 11

Mistakes

Good morning, Lord.
What should a person do
    if she realizes she has made a mistake?
Not lose courage, be more realistic,
    since everyone makes them.
Everyone is human, so bad judgments happen.
I have to become wiser each day,
    profiting by the mistakes I make.
Mistakes help to keep me down to earth.
Mistakes can even bring me closer to people
    if I'm honest with them and myself.
Laughing at mistakes can be a good idea, too.
And then, praying for your guidance, Lord,
    will level the path of pleasing you. Amen.

February 12

My Monotonous Life

Good morning, Lord.
Help me to be patient in routine matters.
I do so many things over and over again,
    and there's no thrill to this monotony.
Even though I'm creative and inquisitive,
    some boring repetition is inescapable:
    the commute to work, zillions of dishes washed,
    food shopping, checkbook balanced,
    sheets laundered, reports completed.
Realistically I can't expect adventure, romance,
    and the extraordinary every hour of the day.
But may I experience satisfaction in knowing
    that I am doing ordinary things
    extraordinarily well. Amen.

Challenge of Loving

Good morning, Lord.
As you view the world at a glance,
    are you pleased with your family?
Have we changed, improved, Lord?
Do we respect one another,
    love one another to the point of sacrifice?
Today, wars, greed, violence,
    and violations of human rights
    are everywhere.
Millions of our brothers and sisters starve,
    trapped in the vicious cycle of poverty,
    and some of us hardly notice.
Look upon the good
    that is done in your name. Amen.

True Love

Good morning, Lord.
For some reason, I was thinking of all those
    who will decide today to marry.
Men and women have fallen in love
    and want to spend all their days with each other
    and live "happily ever after."
Bless them and inspire them to make wise choices.
Let them grasp that love
    means saying "I'm sorry" often,
    calls for commitment and perseverance,
    that marriage is a wedding
    of minds and hearts
    "for better or for worse, for richer or for poorer,
    in sickness and in health." Amen.

Capacity to Love
Good morning, Lord.
You created me with the capacity to love.
They say it makes the world go round.
May I love you first, Lord, above all,
    and love all others because of you.
Help me to know love's real meaning:
It is kind, gentle, and patient;
    it overcomes hatred and evil;
    it wants to give, not just receive;
    it wants to lose oneself in the love of another;
    it wants to forgive.
Let love make my world go round. Amen.

Confidence
Good morning, Lord.
How good it is to talk with you
    at the start of a new day.
Who knows what this day will bring?
Whatever happens,
    let it be with your blessing.
May I walk along your path
    through all the hours of this day.
I begin the day with confidence
    because I know you are with me.
Thank you for helping me
    to realize your constant presence.
Help me to see more of you
    in the events of my life.
Your love and your strength
    keep me going. Amen.

Contentment

Good morning, Lord.
Why am I always dashing off
    to find happiness someplace else?
Maybe today I can just notice
    the people and opportunities at hand.
Perhaps I've seen them a thousand times.
This time I have to open my eyes
    to appreciate the here and now,
    which is all I really have.
Contentment is often elusive.
I am so anxious to search somewhere else
    that I miss the riches along the way.
Thank you, Lord, for helping me to see
    what has been right in front of me. Amen.

Moral Good

Good morning, Lord.
In the beginning you saw
    that all your creation was good.
You called me into existence
    to praise you and give you glory
    by relating to you, others, and the world
    in the fullness of love.
This is your plan for creation:
    your reign of justice and love
    and my happiness
    found in doing your will.
Teach me your ways.
Lord, may you look on me today
    and see what is good in me. Amen.

February 19
Happy People
Good morning, Lord.
I hope I meet happy people today.
Everyone needs people in their lives
    who possess the soft glow of peace.
They make the world a better place
    by their joyous spirit,
    their positive outlook,
    the spark that comes from within them.
Perhaps everyone isn't capable
    of radiating such inner contentment.
Well, perhaps they can try—
    and so can I!
All they need is a charge of confidence
    in your presence. Amen.

February 20
Perspective
Good morning, Lord.
Starting a day with you
    gives me perspective.
Because you gave me life
    and my final destiny is you,
    all the details of the day—
    the happy and sad incidents,
    the challenges and new encounters—
    fall into place.
People are so absorbed with "now"
    that they lose sight of the big picture.
Let me always remember
    to begin and end my day
    with you, Lord. Amen.

Decisions

Good morning, Lord.
"I really don't know what to do."
How often have I said that to myself?
Decisions, moral judgments have to be made,
    but all the information isn't available.
Not to act is sometimes a decision in itself.
Even with our marvelous computers,
    decisions are still not always clear or easy.
I suppose it is a constant reminder
    that we have to search ceaselessly
    for the right way—for you.
We have to keep looking to you, Lord, our light.
I guess that's the way it should be. Amen.

Hearing

Good morning, Lord.
Sounds are all around us,
    welcome and unwelcome.
We listen to birdsong and the voice of a loved one,
    but overhead jets and trucks changing gears
    intrude on our privacy.
Is there any place today
    where sweet silence may be found?
The neighbor may not appreciate
    hard rock blasting from the stereo,
    or even 19th-century opera for that matter.
May we be considerate of the sensitivities of others,
    their desire for welcome sounds.
Thank you for your gift of hearing.
May we respect it in ourselves and in others. Amen.

February 23
Plan of Creation
Good morning, Lord.
Another day and I look out at the world
   to see if the sky is blue and the sun is shining.
Our Earth—
   the mountains, lakes, valleys, deserts—
   has been here for countless centuries.
Now this is my time, my span of years,
   to live on our delicate planet.
And everything has a purpose,
   and I have mine.
The brilliance of your plan of creation, Lord,
   is breathtaking.
Let me know how I may serve—
   you, others, and all Earth inhabitants.
Let me do your will. Amen.

February 24
Worries
Good morning, Lord.
I need your help today.
You see, I woke up with this worry,
   a problem nudging my innards.
I know everyone has problems.
In time, it will go away
   and in two weeks I may not even remember it.
But another will replace it.
These worries keep me in touch with you.
They keep me off balance sometimes, too.
I have to develop an attitude
   that keeps me cool, at peace, and daily reassured.
I've got you, Lord. That's assurance enough. Amen.

People as They Are

Good morning, Lord.
Help me today to deal with people as they are.
We are all at some stage of development.
Let me listen carefully for the clues,
     the interests, concerns, and cries of those I meet.
They may be subtly expressed
     by a little child, a high school student,
     a nursing home resident, a police officer.
Through all the hellos, goodbyes, and pleasantries,
     they may be telling me something
     personal about themselves:
     their feelings, needs, frustrations, challenges.
There are so many ways for me to love another.
Make me more alert and sensitive, Lord. Amen.

God's Love

Good morning, Lord.
Praise and honor to you.
So often I begin my prayer by thinking of myself:
     my moods, my needs.
I tell you all about my life and its challenges,
     as if you weren't already aware.
So today, because of your refreshing grace,
     let me acknowledge you as my Lord and Master,
     my loving, caring God,
     generous and forgiving,
     one who magnanimously has put up with
     my tepid allegiance for so long.
The thought of your love
     gives me courage for the new day. Amen.

February 27
Ups and Downs
Good morning, Lord.
Sometimes I feel all charged up with energy.
At other times I feel like I'm all washed out.
It's not always easy to get it all together.
My moods are often like the fickle weather.
But you are my strength, Lord,
    my stability, my rock.
Let me rejoice in good times and in bad,
    praise you in sunshine and in storms,
    remain faithful through good fortune and bad.
The gift of faith and your grace sustain me,
    and you strengthen me, Lord. Amen.

February 28
Imagination
Good morning, Lord.
You have blessed me with a creative faculty:
    my imagination.
Inspire me to use it productively today.
It can help me meet challenges,
    solve dilemmas,
    find doors to solutions,
    create beauty.
In this extraordinary age of computers
    we find answers quickly, accurately.
Our new discoveries encourage us
    to seek for even more.
The potential, Lord, was there from the start;
    getting it together was simply a process.
For all blessings, especially my imagination,
I thank you. Amen.

Youth

Good morning, Lord.
Bless our young people this day.
Give them grace, understanding, perception
    as they work their way
    through this difficult period.
They are searching for happiness, like us.
Perspectives change over time,
    and they look at life from new angles.
As they seek their fortune, reach for the stars,
    may they discover, Lord,
    that you are the beginning and end of all things.
Our souls are restless,
    until they rest in you, Lord. Amen.

One Family

Good morning, Lord.
There are so many people in our world,
    several billions: men, women, and children.
And there are such differences among us—
    languages, cultures, colors.
We live in different climates—
    on mountains, in the plains, within deep forests,
    concentrated in large cities, all around Earth:
    Alaska, Singapore, Madagascar, Vermont.
But you see us all, Lord, in one glance.
You love us all, individually and personally.
Despite the many differences,
    we are all your children, one family.
May we love one another as you love us. Amen.

"Whatever You Do . . ."

Good morning, Lord.
Some people have much, some very little.
Our supermarkets are filled,
    while, across the seas, our brothers and sisters
    are shackled in the chains of poverty,
    scratching out a living
    with scarce food, shelter, and clothing.
Lord, I hear your words:
"Whatever you do for one of these,
    the least of my brethren, you do to me."
Until we succeed in reaching
    our brothers and sisters in distress,
    our consciences will not be at rest.
Lord, we pray for those in need. Amen.

March 3
Communicators

Good morning, Lord.
For all broadcasters and communicators, we pray.
For the men and women in the public eye
   and those behind the scenes—
   engineers, graphic artists, film editors—
   we beg your blessing.
News, discoveries, achievements, literature
   are communicated everywhere
   with ease and speed.
The broadcaster, the editor, the TV producer:
May they be wise and caring.
Bless their human judgments
   so that the fruit of their work
   may be for the benefit of all. Amen.

March 4
God's Vantage

Good morning, Lord.
The sun is in the sky.
Light blesses our sight and we move about—
   working, playing, eating, singing,
   blessing, and encouraging.
I think of how it must be, Lord,
   for you to see us and be with us
   as we go about our chores
   on farms, in offices, and homes,
   driving along, playing sports, caring for the sick.
How pleased you must be to see
   so many loving one another and remembering you,
   our God, Creator, and Giver of all good gifts.
We thank you. Amen.

Loving Response

Good morning, Lord.
Praise and honor to you in this new day.
Let all my actions and decisions merit your approval.
Accept this day as it is,
    with its joys, its challenges,
    its mistakes and successes.
May it all be to your glory.
Let my conscious and unconscious acts
    be according to your holy will.
You have made me to know you,
    to love you, and to serve you.
May the love and generosity you lavish upon me
    inspire me to love you in return. Amen.

Willing Listener

Good morning, Lord.
No microphones are needed, no headsets,
    no satellite relays to speak to you.
I simply lift up my mind and heart
    wherever I may be and I speak to you.
Prayer is so simple, easy conversation
    and there is no more willing a listener,
    no more concerned person than you, Lord.
Just pleasant conversation.
I thank you this morning for my faith,
    for the grace and blessing to know how to pray,
    to approach you in deepest humility.
You are my kind, loving father.
Hallowed be your name.
May your kingdom come. Amen.

March 7

Attitude

Good morning, Lord.
Let me be gracious today,
    meeting uncertainties and unpleasant moments
    with unflappable courtesy.
We are all called to maintain good public relations.
With that extra effort, that charge of motivation,
    I can smile at the testy waiter,
    the high-strung executive,
    the impetuous, horn-honking motorist.
Being gracious is like going through and around
    the day's inevitable obstacles without collision,
    without an infuriating head-to-head confrontation.
Attitude, Lord, attitude.
Help me to be gracious to all I meet today. Amen.

March 8

Teach Me Many Things

Good morning, Lord.
Teach me many things this day.
Through instructors, books, television, people,
    let me learn how to grow as a person.
Dispose my mind and my heart
    to be sensitive, receptive.
It is so interesting to learn,
    to discover people, places, and things,
    and see them all in fresh relationships.
And let me learn of you, Lord,
    by studying the works of your creation:
    colorful flowers, lofty mountains,
    rushing streams, and beautiful people.
Let me learn of you. Amen.

Real Beauty

Good morning, Lord.
There are many ads and commercials
  on how to be beautiful.
Millions are spent on products
  that are supposed to enhance one's glamor.
Can beauty really come about
  with creams, lotions, potions, colors, and styles?
Maybe they accentuate good features
  or perhaps highlight physical attributes.
Is not there an inner beauty in each person?
Many times we come to appreciate
  a person's qualities, their inner beauty.
Everyone is beautiful after your image, Lord.
We pray for the grace to appreciate this. Amen.

All Passing By

Good morning, Lord.
I have the feeling that nothing is permanent.
All is transitory, passing us by:
  the seasons, nature's world, and us, your people.
The experience is more dramatic at times:
  winter snows melt into rushing streams,
  barren branches sprout leaves,
  grandfathers die, and babies are born.
Actually, it is a beautiful experience.
Your world changes marvelously before us,
  and we are drawn to you.
We find our strength, our consolation,
and our foundation in you,
  our unchanging God and destiny. Amen.

March 11
In a Spin
Good morning, Lord.
Daily I wake to a world on the move:
    people, places, things in constant flow.
Our planet is in a spin
    and we are going for a ride.
There is nostalgia for what was,
    a wishful thinking
        that we might capture life in a freeze frame,
        perhaps pleasant times never to be modified.
All of this may be delightful, but unrealistic.
We pray to be compatible, Lord,
    with life's inevitable rhythm,
        to grow gracefully in our environment.
May we keep our balance as we move along. Amen.

March 12
Compliments
Good morning, Lord.
Let me not hesitate to compliment my friends,
    to praise my relatives and acquaintances.
I hesitate at times to do so.
Maybe they'll think I'm after something,
    flattering them before asking for a loan.
Perhaps I hesitate to tell someone
    how good she is at sports,
    at cooking, at negotiating, or writing verse,
    as if I will lose something of myself
    by giving away praise and appreciation.
I should say, "You're a good mechanic,"
    or, "I like the way you relate to people."
For the grace to say it out loud, I pray. Amen.

A Good Listener

Good morning, Lord.
Let me be attentive today to those who speak to me,
    the way I expect you to hang on my every word.
So often the sounds and syllables reach us,
    but we fail to grasp the real message.
Good listeners are appreciated.
Even little children brighten up and respond
    when they see us paying attention to them.
Many times we say yes, or no, or grunt, or nod,
    but our lack of genuine interest is transparent.
That's the bottom line: truly caring,
    caring enough to listen with feeling
    when anyone speaks to us.
We pray for this grace this day. Amen.

Getting Started

Good morning, Lord.
Some days I just can't get started.
"How come I was so full of ambition yesterday
    and today I'm a person in slow motion?"
The human condition suffers many moods.
It is alive and reacts to climate, to surroundings,
    and even to the remarks of friends.
Help me, Lord, to maintain an even keel
    in all kinds of weather,
    a calm, balanced disposition.
Storms pass, squalls rise and die out,
    and the bright sunshine returns
    to gladden our hearts.
Keep me going, Lord. Amen.

March 15

The Grace of Faith

Good morning, Lord.
Thank you for all my blessings,
    but especially for my faith.
I believe in you, Lord.
These are not empty words.
You know all things and call me to yourself.
Still there are millions of men and women
    in our own land not blessed with the gift of faith.
They rise and toil, eat and sleep,
    seemingly unmindful of your caring presence.
It is bewildering how creatures
    can be oblivious of their creator.
May they be blessed with a fertile mind and heart
    and share in the precious grace of faith. Amen.

March 16

God's Will

Good morning, Lord.
Let me begin this new day full of trust in you.
I am in your hands.
Bless all my words and actions.
You have given me a mind and a will.
It's another day to decide
    where to go, what to say and do.
I feel a certain independence;
I am the "master of my fate, the captain of my soul."
Favor me with understanding and insight.
Let me embrace your will as my guide,
    as my standard of right and wrong,
    the compass of my decisions.
Thy will be done, Lord, on Earth. Amen.

Great Expectation

Good morning, Lord.
There is nothing like a face-to-face encounter.
People say, "You look so different from your pictures."
Or, "I never realized you were so handsome."
Actors are known one way on the screen,
     but in still another way in person.
"Getting to know you" may be a song to sing,
     but in reality an encounter is indispensable for this.
An encounter is needed to really know someone.
One day, Lord, we expect to meet you face to face.
We see you now, as St. Paul says, "in a mirror."
For now, the reflections of our world
     tell us of your love, majesty, and fidelity.
Thank you, Lord, for this anticipation. Amen.

God's Works

Good morning, Lord.
Help us to recognize your greatness in your works.
Let us see your artistry in golden sunsets,
     in the riot of color in autumn leaves,
     in the downpour of a rain forest,
     in the complex coordination
     of our muscles, cells, bones, blood, and spirit, too.
We come to know an author
     through the evidence of her writing.
Let us know you, Lord,
     through the many blessings of your world,
     the work of your hands.
Grant us the grace to recognize you in your works,
     to appreciate your abiding presence. Amen.

March 19

Crime

Good morning, Lord.
There are days when I awake feeling helpless,
    that certain things are beyond me,
    and I can do nothing to change them.
Crime, for example.
Criminals and wanton violence today
    are as tenacious, as pervasive, as destructive
    as cancer in society's system.
We do not have a cure for this moral sickness.
But I know, Lord, that you are more powerful,
    that your grace turns hearts of stone
    into hearts of flesh,
        even of the most determined criminal. Amen.

March 20

"As Little Children"

Good morning, Lord.
For all the children in our world, I pray.
The girls and boys whose hearts are pure,
    whose minds are open—
    may they never be spoiled.
The little child has a mystique, an attraction,
    a spirit that you favor.
Is it the trust in their eyes? Their openness?
Is it their unabashed eagerness to be loved
    and to love all others?
They open their arms
    confident they will be welcomed,
    and they disarm the world.
We are to "become as little children."
Help us all to learn from them. Amen.

More than Appearances

Good morning, Lord.
My eyes are opened. I'm awake now.
Help me to see more than appearances today.
I want to notice signs of spring,
  be aware of the wonders of nature,
  the raindrops, the budding trees, the cool winds.
Most of all, let me be aware of other people,
  loved by you, made after your image.
Teach me to love my neighbor.
I want to realize how lovable
  are the young, the old, the blacks, the whites,
  everyone you love.
Thanks again for this new day,
  and for the new opportunity. Amen.

Money and God

Good morning, Lord.
"I don't need a million dollars,"
  a song begins, "to make my dreams come true."
The pursuit of money is sometimes
  a consuming and empty quest.
We all know it cannot buy happiness.
The song continues, "All I need is you."
How often I have reminded myself
  of this rock-bottom wisdom,
  and then gone on to lust for treasures.
I have to struggle to keep things in perspective.
All created, material things are good,
  but always a means to an end.
Our souls are restless for you, Lord. Amen.

March 23
Present Moment
Good morning, Lord.
This is a day like no other day.
It is the only one I have.
The past is gone, the future has not arrived.
Bless me and let me appreciate
    the grace of the present moment.
I wish to look outward today,
    to see the goodness and beauty in other people,
    to see your footprints in nature's handiwork.
Let me not spend an unproductive day,
    taken up with the usual worries and cares.
My personal troubles, real or imaginary,
    melt like frost in the sunshine of loving others.
For this beautiful day, thank you, Lord. Amen.

March 24
A Day's Blessings
Good morning, Lord.
Thank you for all the blessings of this day.
I cannot look clearly into the future,
    but I know good things will happen
    because of your love, kindness, and concern.
Why must I often remind myself of this?
Your simple message has always been
    "I love you."
The evidence is all around me.
May I recognize your favors, your grace in my life.
Let me be appreciative,
    full of gratitude for having so wonderful a God.
Open my eyes and my heart, Lord,
    to the limitless expressions of your love. Amen.

A Few Good Laughs

Good morning, Lord.
Let me have a few good laughs today.
At times I have a feeling
    that my problems and responsibilities
    are becoming manageable, falling into place.
The weight I have felt from them
    may dissipate with a good laugh or two.
This makes me wonder
    how much of life's burden is real or imaginary.
Besides, who wants to associate
    with Gloomy Gus or Sour Sally?
May I recognize your love and blessing
    in balanced humor, Lord.
You've got the whole world in your hands. Amen.

Managing Challenges

Good morning, Lord.
For all who awake discouraged, we pray.
May they turn to you
    and find joy, peace, and renewed spirit.
No one walks alone.
All challenges are manageable.
There is no problem that you and they
    cannot handle together.
Lord, you give up on no one,
    and we should not give up on you.
We need the simple, childlike trust of children.
With faith we all can move
    the mountains of our worries.
I love you, Lord, and I believe in you. Amen.

March 27
Global Vision
Good morning, Lord.
Help me not to be shortsighted,
   globally speaking.
It's a big world, wide and wonderful.
Millions of people on every continent,
   with lovely customs and traditions to share.
Those who travel often return enriched,
   realizing how much there is to see and learn.
Help me always to appreciate
   the wisdom, the diversity, the difference,
   in nationality and in individual character.
Every person in the world is unique,
   special to you, Lord, and, I pray, to me, too.
For your enlightenment, we pray. Amen.

March 28
Foolish Moments
Good morning, Lord.
I have a special request this new day.
Please help me in my foolish moments.
I do behave foolishly on occasion,
   incidents when I act out-of-character,
   say regrettable words, act impetuously,
   because I don't stop to think or pray a bit.
Maybe it's when I get very angry,
   or when there is pressure from a deadline.
On other occasions I am so high and happy
   that I could hug everyone in sight.
Keep me steady, Lord.
Bless me when my judgment is only too human.
Thank you for watching over me. Amen.

Praying from Strength

Good morning, Lord.
Help me through this day.
I do not pray from weakness, weak as I am.
I pray from strength
  because I know your great love for me.
My challenges, my trials, and temptations
  are opportunities to respond to your love.
Your ways are mysterious, Lord,
  but I must never doubt
  your constant presence and love.
There is no reason for me not to be
  optimistic and confident.
Trust is a key to positive living.
Instill this in me, Lord, this day. Amen.

Anxieties

Good morning, Lord.
Help me to break loose
  from my usual chain of anxieties.
Life at times is a circle and I discover myself
  coming around to last week's troubles.
I haven't yet become a carefree child of God,
  skipping through life hand in hand with you.
But this day is going to be different.
The silly cycle of gnawing concerns
  is already interrupted.
You are my rock, my refuge, my strength.
There will be no dark, foreboding valleys
  because you are at my side.
Thank you, Lord, for your sustaining love. Amen.

March 31

Appreciating Values

Good morning, Lord.

Scales and computers, weights and measures
    help us to determine weights and numbers
    but it takes a mind, a spirit to appreciate values.
Films, songs, so much of our society,
    like the biblical serpent in the garden,
    may tell us that there is happiness in sin.
We discover to our loss and regret
    that forbidden fruit tastes sour.
It churns our innards, gives us no peace.
Lord, may we learn values from your word:
    goodness, kindness, patience, justice,
    purity, fidelity, honesty, respect.
There are no substitutes for these. Amen.

Make Someone Happy

Good morning, Lord.
What will this day bring?
Before I lie down to sleep,
 what experiences are in store for me?
The sensational and explosive?
The routine and expected?
It will be a productive day, I know,
 if I am closer to you,
 if I have been kind and considerate,
 if I have forgotten numero uno for a change.
How is it written?
"A cup of water given in your name . . ."
Let me be as generous today
 as I imagine myself to be. Amen.

A Day's Promise

Good morning, Lord.
Every new day holds out promise.
A better world is in store; fulfillment beckons.
Lord, within us all there is a longing,
 a hunger and thirst for contentment.
Help me not to search in vain
 down the wrong paths, into enticing by-ways
 that lead to frustration and misery.
You are the good Shepherd.
Following you, I shall not stray.
Help me to know your will,
 esteem your teachings, cherish your commands.
It is you I seek, Lord, or else my soul is restless.
Destiny, happiness, your presence, Lord. Amen.

April 3
Seeking Answers
Good morning, Lord.
History makes plain we don't have all the answers.
We've waged wars on all continents,
    evidence of our inability or unwillingness
    to solve disputes nonviolently.
We do not hold the cures to some diseases.
We do not know how to feed, clothe,
    and shelter all people everywhere.
Simply, we don't know how to love effectively.
Grant us wisdom and understanding.
Show us the way to a better life
    through research, cooperation, dialogue,
    all the while consumed with good will.
Let us discover your holy will in our day. Amen.

April 4
Restlessness
Good morning, Lord.
For all of us restless people, we pray.
Some of us keep looking over hills,
    thinking happiness lies on the other side.
We are not downright discontent,
    yet seem to be in constant search.
There is a fire within that flares,
    dies down, but never stops smoldering.
Persons, places, things—
    we go mindlessly from one to the other.
May we set goals and try to achieve them.
Channel our restlessness into productive activity,
    and grant us peace of mind, Lord,
    and holy purposefulness. Amen.

Opportunity

Good morning, Lord.
I thank you for this new day.
With hope and confidence, Lord,
I begin living these precious hours,
    time you give me to enjoy—and improve—
    your wonderful world.
The scriptures comment on the work of creation:
"God saw that it was good,"
    and this is a good day, a good world.
Thank you for the opportunity
    to recognize your love in creation this day.
You are not far from me, Lord.
May I walk with you this day
    according to your holy will. Amen.

Beside Restful Waters

Good morning, Lord.
We've all heard the chatter of birds,
    their excited tweeting before the sun rises.
Before jets, trains, and cars,
    before diesel rigs and bikes with rotten mufflers,
    mornings had gentler waking sounds.
Many of us still enjoy sound waves
    undiluted with mechanical din.
The simple things in life are still available.
In an often complicated world,
    we long for the quiet lakeside, the solitary walk,
    the tranquil glen, the empty beach.
Help us, Lord, to retreat a little, to find you.
Beside your restful waters let us find repose. Amen.

April 7
Friendship

Good morning, Lord.
I pray for my friends today,
   those who share their lives with me.
May I always be a good friend,
   seeking to please others,
   taking interest in their work and ideas,
   sympathetic to their feelings and sensitivities.
When we meet, their greetings lift my spirits.
Friendship is an elixir, a delightful part of life.
Let me be open to new friends.
In time I may discover how blessed I am,
   how much I have received from friendship.
And may the friendship of your love, Lord,
   be a source of joy this day. Amen.

April 8
Daily Offering

Good morning, Lord.
I offer you this day:
   all my thoughts, words, and actions.
May all my waking hours please you.
What, after all, can I give except what I have:
   my life, as simple and unpretentious as it is.
May my efforts to do ordinary tasks well
   win favor in your sight.
I pray that I may see goodness
   in all the people I meet,
   that I may be aware of your great love for them.
Strengthen me by your grace
   to overcome my weaknesses.
May your holy will find fulfillment in my life. Amen.

Faith

Good morning, Lord.
There is power in faith.
Faith is like a bridge between heaven and Earth,
    between ourselves and you.
It cannot be measured on a scale
    or touched with a hand.
It is a spiritual power, an inner strength.
My faith rests in you, Lord,
    who hear my every word
    and have power to aid me.
In my darkest hours, it sustains me.
It is a positive force that links me to you.
Thank you, Lord, for this wonderful gift.
May I share my faith with others. Amen.

Forgiving God

Good morning, Lord.
There are times when I'm reading
    that lines leap from the page at me:
    such as, "I do not condemn you,
    go, and from now on, avoid this sin."
Comforting words to the adulterous woman.
When I'm down and nearly out,
    when I'm not pleased with myself,
    when guilt and shame well up in my heart,
I need to think of your loving forgiveness.
Everyone bears the burden of personal sin,
    everyone struggles with guilty feelings,
    and everyone needs, above all, to remember
    what kind of a God you are. Amen.

April 11
Open Mind
Good morning, Lord.
Help me to be open, receptive
    to new ideas and new people.
A closed mind, a narrow vision
    does not make for human progress.
"Happy are those who hear the word
    in the spirit of openness;
    they shall bear fruit through perseverance."
Sometimes we typecast another person,
    have biased opinions on another's abilities,
    and limit our appreciation of them.
Let your light shine in, Lord.
Light up my life and my mind,
    and let me be open to your inspiration. Amen.

April 12
Good Health
Good morning, Lord.
Most people live their lives in good health.
The flu bugs, the kidney stones,
    the mumps, and measles restrict our activity
    a small number of days in a long lifetime.
This is not to play down our challenges
    to conquer all illness and provide
    care, love, and service to the afflicted.
But we tend to let the good days pass by,
    fade from memory all too quickly: the afternoons
    at the beach,
    the rounds of golf, the family gatherings.
Looking back, the good things in life
    are not appreciated enough.
Our healthy days are days of blessing. Amen.

Talents

Good morning, Lord.
Everyone has talent.
Help me to develop my talents
    that I may share in your creative process.
People say they have no special talents.
Inspire them with confidence.
Activate their imagination.
Writing, speaking, painting, singing, playing—
    there is so much glory to be given,
    so much we can do for one another.
We must not set limits on our abilities.
You, after all, have endowed us.
Thank you for my talents,
    and for this promising day. Amen.

Helping One Person

Good morning, Lord.
If I can help just one person,
    it will be a successful day.
There is no need to stand on a corner
    waiting to help a little old woman cross the street.
And I don't have to be a foreign missionary
    to find someone awaiting my services.
There is a shut-in to be visited,
    a child to be taught, a sinner to be prayed for,
    a hungry man to be fed,
    a grieving woman to be consoled,
    an addict to be counseled,
    phone contacts with family to be made.
Let me be an instrument of your love, Lord. Amen.

April 15
Tax Forms
Good morning, Lord.
Bless all the men and women tax preparers.
They review months of expenditures and income,
    deductions, estimations, and depreciations.
Calculators rattle and computers whir.
Look with favor on these experts,
    the professionals and the amateurs,
    all those whose minds are absorbed
    in the laws and mathematics of the season.
Many things in life may be simple,
    but these complicated forms are not.
Assist them to be responsible and honest
    in rendering Caesar his due. Amen.

April 16
Thinking of Others
Good morning, Lord.
Thinking of other people at the start of a day
    gets me out of my introspection.
Bless the postal workers, police officers, fire fighters,
    supermarket clerks, mechanics, garbage collectors,
    chefs, teachers, and maintenance people,
    priests, ministers, deacons, nuns.
Bless all those members of our community
    who work for the good of all.
Each has a part to play in our society,
    making it run smoothly
    for the benefit of all.
May we appreciate the hard work each one does.
What can I do, Lord,
    to make this community a bit better? Amen.

True Parent

Good morning, Lord.
Thank you for another day in my life.
I am blessed in knowing how much you love me.
There are days I wake up thinking
    how insecure I am.
My first impulse is to pray frantically
    for the strength that only you can give.
Then I recall your concern, your interest in me
    and I chide myself.
After all, what kind of a God do I believe in?
Are you not my true parent?
I can do all things in you who strengthen me.
What great peace you instill into my being.
I love you, Lord. Amen.

Silent Presence

Good morning, Lord.
Sometimes I wake up wanting to pray,
    and I just can't focus on anything.
This is one of those mornings.
So I offer you this empty state of mind.
It isn't much, Lord, but it is all that I have.
But even silence can be a form of praise too,
    can't it?
Let me just be here these few moments—
    in your presence.
I'm thinking of you, Lord, with love, with respect.
My thoughts are slow coming,
    but my heart is right.
Bless me Lord, this day. Amen.

April 19

Appreciation

Good morning, Lord.
Thank you for another day.
I must never forget
    that you are the giver of all good gifts.
I live and move and have my being
    because of your love and generosity.
Everything I have I owe to you:
    my body, my talents, my family,
    my friends, this wonderful land.
I pray that I may always appreciate
    your many blessings.
And there will be more to thank you for,
    when the sun sets.
My good and gracious God, thank you. Amen.

April 20

Humble of Heart

Good morning, Lord.
Your words leap from the page:
"Learn from me for I am meek and humble of heart."
This precious quality eludes me often.
Being meek and humble of heart
    is a very pleasing and attractive way to be.
A personality has depth and quality
    when meekness and humility are present,
    when they glow from a mature character.
They contrast with the boastful and brassy.
But those who are meek and humble
    are so easy to love and close to you.
Like you, Lord:
    This special grace I pray for. Amen.

Mother Earth

Good morning, Lord.
I look out on planet Earth again
    and recall the poet's words:
"O world, I cannot hold thee close enough."
I am occupied with my work, running errands,
    watching TV, paying bills.
I become daily absorbed in details,
    caught up in a busy, fast-moving world.
Thank you for this occasion to pause
    and reflect on where I am,
    on the beauty of my home,
    on all my brothers and sisters in creation.
Lord, let me see my part in the environment. Amen.

Secretaries

Good morning, Lord.
For all the secretaries in the thousands of offices
I pray this day.
Women mostly, but men too,
    organize voluminous data,
    take notes, keep communications humming,
    and keep operations on schedule.
Their fingers fly over computer keyboards
    producing countless pages of copy.
For all the good secretaries—
    may they be up to the challenges of each day.
We thank you and ask your blessing on them
Make them even more efficient.
May we reward them with appreciation
    and with equality. Amen.

April 23
Spiritual Life

Good morning, Lord.
May I always be interested
   in the spiritual welfare of others,
     to encourage them and lift their sagging spirits.
Lonely neighbors would beam
   if I brought them a homemade pie.
Hospital patients would be cheered
   if I visited them or sent them a card.
Children are encouraged when I praise their drawings.
When I pray with worried folks,
   you come and strengthen their spirit.
And, Lord, if I may assist someone
   in their quest for eternal happiness,
   let me somehow be your instrument. Amen.

April 24
Gardeners and Florists

Good morning, Lord.
My prayer today is for gardeners and florists.
They bring such color and happiness into our lives.
They till the soil to produce
   a riot of reds and yellows, lavenders and pinks.
Whether commercial or from the backyard,
   the sprays and arrangements
   gladden hearts on a wedding day;
   they communicate comfort and solace
   to those saddened by death and separation;
   they provide buds and blossoms for the sick.
Bless all who labor to bring us
   the flowers you cause to grow.
Let us all appreciate your handiwork, Lord. Amen.

Good Judgment

Good morning, Lord.
Bless this day with good judgment.
May every decision be a good one.
The buck does stop here; that's the bottom line.
While your wisdom is unquestionable
    and your will is to be done,
    we stumble, make mistakes,
    and continue to blunder through with our errors.
Inspire us and flood our minds with light
    and give strength to our wills.
May our motivation always be unselfish.
We seek to please you by serving one another.
Surely, Lord, all things work together
    toward good for those who love you. Amen.

Commandments

Good morning, Lord.
Let me see great blessing and wisdom
    in your commandments.
If I ignore them, see them as unwarranted restrictions
    or so many shackles to my freedom,
I may think of you as my disciplinarian,
    instead of as my caring Father.
You express your will in a clear manner, Lord,
    to guide me in the way of freedom.
Your commands are for everyone, everywhere,
    in all centuries and in all seasons.
In them I discover right and wrong.
Teach me to love and respect others, Lord,
    by keeping your commandments. Amen.

April 27
Positive Thinking

Good morning, Lord.
I'll start the day saying I know I can do anything.
Thinking positively is the only way to live.
Of course, I must not want to do anything
    you don't want me to do.
I know that sometimes I engage in wishful thinking.
I'd like to play a musical instrument,
    speak another language, write a book.
Dreams and more dreams?
I have to be practical: learn the musical scales,
    memorize words, write a few lines.
After that, it's just determination and perseverance—
    well, maybe some self-confidence, too.
Bless all of us positive thinkers, Lord. Amen.

April 28
Good for Evil

Good morning, Lord.
St. Paul's advice is
"If your enemy is hungry, feed him;
    if he is thirsty, give him something to drink."
It is the ancient counsel:
Never repay injury with injury
    but conquer evil with good.
How often have we seen national policies
    reversed even in our lifetime.
We warred against the Germans, now our allies.
We are welcoming Vietnamese to our shores.
We forget, and then have to relearn
    that love must eventually succeed.
This is your way, Lord. Amen.

As a Child

Good morning, Lord.
Thank heaven for little girls and boys,
 the sweet innocence of children.
They embody a quality blessed by yourself:
"Unless you become like little children,
 you shall not enter the kingdom of heaven."
It is a grand simplicity, this childlike spirit,
 an unencumbered directness.
That quality of life is the entrance fee
 to lasting happiness.
It is a reminder of the way I ought to be:
 unsophisticated, undisguised, unadulterated.
Thank you for this grace, this insight,
 this wonderful new day of childlikeness. Amen.

Creativity

Good morning, Lord.
Help me never to grow "too old to dream."
Who says there is a cut-off date
 on inspiration and creative thought?
The imagination is a marvelous faculty
 coloring our world, dusting it with magic.
It needs exercise, priming, and freedom.
Some folks reach an age when they think
 they have made their contribution to society
 and the expected thing to do is fade away.
We draw from the wellspring of your creativity, Lord.
We are never too old to meet new challenges,
 never powerless with your grace.
Thank you for this new day and insight. Amen.

The Godless

Good morning, Lord.
How reassuring it is
   when the sun breaks through an overcast day.
It changes everything.
It's like you, Lord, coming into our lives.
(How empty, a life without faith.)
It's like being in love
   and separated from a lover.
Peace and contentment come in knowing you.
You are love, and make life worth living.
Shower the godless with your grace.
Penetrate stony hearts
   with the sunlight of love.
Help us to share our faith with others.
Your generosity should be communicated. Amen.

Uptight

Good morning, Lord.
Sometimes I want to lie down,
   look at the blue sky, and laugh and laugh.
How seriously I take life,
   trying so hard to make things happen—just so!
I recall the lines about your care and concern
   for the birds of the sky, the lilies of the field,
   how they neither sow nor reap
   but have you watching over them.
Then I laugh at silly me.
Is it not futile to be so uptight,
   so overly intent and humorless?
I trust in you, loving God. Amen.

May 3
Religious People
Good morning, Lord.
For all priests, religious brothers,
sisters, ministers, clergy of all faiths,
we ask your grace and blessing.
Some say, "Oh, they don't need our prayers."
But everyone depends upon you, loving God.
For all their sincerity, they are often misunderstood.
Missionaries who sacrifice comfort, family,
friends, and homeland
are sometimes scalded with criticism.
They may work to be instruments of your peace,
but find themselves embroiled in controversy.
Give them light, courage, and fidelity.
Like us, they are human and challenged. Amen.

May 4
Interior Peace
Good morning, Lord.
Bless me with peace today, truly content.
May I realize that you are with me.
My days are often busy, so frantic.
I long for a quiet place beside a stream,
where the gentle rhythm of the waters
works its way into my charged emotions.
Time to reflect, to size up life's circumstances,
to see there really is logic and order.
Business people pressure themselves
to accomplish more than the day allows.
All of us on this whirling planet
are in need of that peace, that tranquility
We need to rediscover your loving care. Amen.

God's Presence

Good morning, Lord.
Let me realize your presence
   throughout this day.
As I answer phones, commute to work,
   exchange greetings, eat lunch,
   let me be mindful of your presence.
My attitude is not "I know you're watching,
   so I better be good."
But there ought to be that secure feeling,
   the awareness that you are with me.
I do forget, becoming absorbed in details,
   but as the song says, "I'll never walk alone."
Help me to reflect on your sustaining power,
   your constant care and concern. Amen.

Faith

Good morning, Lord.
Thank you for the gift of faith.
It seems I appreciate it more each day.
To be able to believe is a grace.
Without having encountered you face to face,
I believe with confidence and conviction.
Millions live without a rich dimension in their lives.
To them, the end of life is meaningless;
   it is the beginning of nothingness.
You have revealed yourself,
   and I accept what you say about yourself.
Let my mind and heart be open to your word,
   wherever it may be found.
To believe is a precious gift. Thank you. Amen.

May 7

Repentance

Good morning, Lord.
You have often forgiven me my sins;
I am overwhelmed by your mercy.
If someone crossed me as often as I crossed you,
    they would be dealing with a fellow
    with paper-thin patience and an angry fist.
How can you absorb so many offenses
    and still come up loving?
It makes me sick of myself at times,
    and I come up determined not to sin again.
That's what makes the difference.
You are my ever-loving God,
    and I'll confess that I'm your repentant sinner.
Thank you, Lord, for your peace. Amen.

May 8

God's Guidance

Good morning, Lord.
Every day I pray for moral wisdom.
This day brings the challenge of new decisions.
While you have blessed me with the power
    of free will to make independent judgments,
I realize only too well my need to be guided.
You, Lord, are the Truth, and speak infallibly,
    and I am constantly subject to mistakes,
    to selfishness, even to sin.
Help me not to hesitate in my decision making
    because of weakness.
After I have searched hard for the truth,
    prayed, and accepted counsel,
    let my will conform to yours, Lord. Amen.

Faithful to Promises

Good morning, Lord.
Help us all to be faithful to our promises.
If we have given our word,
 strengthen us to fulfill it.
Let not our promises be dismissed lightly;
 it is a pledge of ourselves.
Those who receive our promises find assurance,
 live in hope, trust in our love.
May the promises of brides and grooms
 to love and to cherish in good times and in bad
 for richer or for poorer, in sickness or in health,
 be faithfully realized in daily living.
May their vows, made to seal mutual love, be kept
 and mirror your never-ending love for us all. Amen.

Hand in Hand

Good morning, Lord.
Life takes on a different meaning
 when I realize your presence.
Life is more than a series of daily challenges,
 frustrations, trials, and disappointments.
Because of your communication,
 it has purpose, joy, and perspective.
Life does not have an ending, Lord, thanks to you.
We have a happy destiny, sharing your life.
Thank you for your love,
 for the supreme blessing:
I walk hand in hand with you,
 and you care for me in your divine providence.
This is another good day because of you, Lord. Amen.

May 11

The Beauty in All

Good morning, Lord.
Let me recognize good in all people:
    the beautiful and the unattractive,
    the pleasant and the disagreeable.
Even ugly stumps can be carved into shapely statues.
You see the potential in each of us.
You are patient with our blunders,
    and wait for us to get over our selfish ways.
When we come to understand your love for us,
    we grow, we mature, we change.
Help us to have the same view of others.
A little love goes a long way.
Show people confidence and care
    and they rise to the occasion.
For the grace to see beauty in everyone,
    and for this new day to do so, thank you. Amen.

May 12

A Favored Life

Good morning, Lord.
I'm in a very quiet, reflective mood,
    thinking how favored I've been all my life.
The good times far outnumber the bad.
There are so few sick days
    compared to the years of good health.
I've sat down to unappetizing meals,
    but I recall the thousands of good ones.
I take the air I breathe and the friends I meet—
    I take so much for granted.
I'm making gratitude my special prayer.
Your grace hit me this morning:
    "What do I have that I haven't received?"
Forgive me for my past indifference. Amen.

From Needs to Knees

Good morning, Lord.
Many of us turn to you in our distress.
Confronted with problems, suffering and weak,
    we become discouraged and turn to prayer.
Often our desperation brings us closer to you.
Help us all to appreciate the power of prayer.
Prayer is more than "asking";
    it is praising and glorifying your holy name, too.
But our needs bring us to our knees;
    in prayer we rediscover you,
    Lord, your loving kindness,
    your generosity and compassion.
You are the Father who answers our pleas.
Lord, teach us to pray
    with even greater confidence. Amen.

Desperate People

Good morning, Lord.
I pray for all the desperate people in our world.
There must be many, judging from revolutions,
    hostage taking, refugees, and violent crimes.
Hotlines are maintained to help folks
    who feel impelled to do desperate things.
Can we not reach out and share?
We all have to communicate hope to others,
    to motivate those with resources
    to share out of their abundance.
Let no one be complacent
    when brothers and sisters are suffering.
Let your love for us be translated into action. Amen.

Friendship

Good morning, Lord.
Friends are those you like to be with—
    talking, laughing, sharing.
Friends are people on your wavelength,
    in concert with your feelings and ideas.
Friends understand.
And Lord, you are my unchanging friend:
    always close, supportive, dependable, loving.
There is no true relationship with you
    unless I appreciate you as my friend.
Our association is not one of slave and master.
You really do care, Lord.
For all my friends who are so kind to me,
    and for your comforting friendship, thank you.
Amen.

Difficult Moments

Good morning, Lord.
Not knowing what this new day has in store,
    I want to thank you for its difficult moments.
It is only right and fitting to praise you
    in good times as well as in bad.
Life cannot be all sunshine and blue skies.
Husband and wife promise to take one another
    in a lasting relationship, for better or for worse.
Being grateful to you in unpleasant situations,
    on occasions of discouragement or depression,
    is a "turn about" for most of us.
If I have sweet words only when things go well,
    I am losing sight of your love.
You are always with me, Lord. Amen.

Money

Good morning, Lord.
Various attitudes toward life often clash
    as we work our way through life.
Such as, how can I earn the most money
    in the shortest amount of time?
And, blessed are the poor in spirit.
Many live only to accumulate wealth.
Others are content to go fishing by a lazy stream.
They say we can't take our money with us,
    and to sloganize, you can't go anywhere without it.
But the scriptures teach the love of money
    is the root of evil.
Help us to have our hearts in the right place.
Where our treasure is, there our heart will be. Amen.

Justice

Good morning, Lord.
Help me to work for justice.
Justice means being fair and honest,
    giving to each person what is due to them.
No cheating. No skimming or doctoring accounts.
Justice demands respect, a deep conviction
    about the worth of other persons and their rights.
What would happen in our world
    if shoplifters, muggers, accountants, burglars
suddenly had a change of heart?
If they heard a voice from within saying
    you can't rip off my friends?
May we all hear your voice, Lord,
    and treat all others with total honesty. Amen.

May 19

Problems

Good morning, Lord.
I seldom think of thanking you for my quandaries.
I pray long and hard for a solution to my problems.
I pray for wisdom, understanding, enlightenment.
My words fly heavenward
   to relieve me from my misery and distress.
"Nobody knows the troubles I've seen."
But I thank you today for my problems,
   the bewildering circumstances I find myself in.
They provide me with the opportunity
   to turn to you with renewed confidence,
   and to recall your love for me.
From my anguish of heart,
   a closer relationship with you may emerge. Amen.

May 20

Mothers

Good morning, Lord.
I pray this morning for all devoted mothers,
   the millions who love and care for their children.
Being a good mother is a special vocation.
Theirs are qualities beyond loving or disciplining.
Lord, you have blessed mothers
   with a unique sensitivity
   to the unspoken needs of sons and daughters.
Our mothers need to know
   that they are loved and appreciated.
Give them courage, strength, tenderness.
May they trust in you, Lord,
   confident of your loving support.
Their calling is our nation's treasure. Amen.

Parents

Good morning, Lord.
I pray for good mothers and fathers.
Children are our most precious resource.
You give them life in the womb
  and entrust them to the love of their parents.
They are impressionable, pliable, receptive.
Like soft wax, their minds and hearts
  are formed by their parents over the years.
Sustain these mothers and fathers
  in their love for their children.
Let them be mindful of all their children's needs,
  especially their spiritual needs,
    helping them in their growing relationship
    with you, our gracious God. Amen.

Convictions

Good morning, Lord.
Provide me with the courage of my convictions.
Realizing my limitations, my weaknesses,
I need your grace to live up to my ideals.
Let me be honest with myself.
Falling short of noble ambitions
  is an almost inevitable happening.
But as I insist on quality in products,
  let me strive to develop quality in myself.
Being a better person takes time.
My progress may often be imperceptible:
  inch by inch over a thousand-mile journey.
Let me praise you by the sincerity of my life.
Let me honor you by striving all my life
to live according to my convictions. Amen.

May 23
Surgery
Good morning, Lord.
As I pray to you this moment,
   people are preparing to undergo surgery.
Examinations have been made, blood sampled,
   tests done in the laboratories, X-rays taken.
Now medical teams ready themselves:
   doctors, nurses, technicians, counselors.
Give them all skill and compassion.
Provide strength and stamina to the patients.
Dispel their apprehensions,
   and inspire them with courage.
Settle their minds and hearts
   with perfect dispositions to your holy will.
Let them be mindful of your love. Amen.

May 24
Being Afraid
Good morning, Lord.
Sometimes I am afraid, an experience
   that comes upon me without warning.
Life's circumstances slip out of alignment—
   others are full of confidence, moving with poise—
   and I become unglued.
Do you allow me these trying moments
   to keep me humble?
   to keep me from becoming too proud?
   even defiantly independent?
I know all things can work together for good.
My fears disappear with renewed trust in you.
I do forget your constant love for me.
Thank you, Lord, for my beneficial trials. Amen.

Glorifying God

Good morning, Lord.
Let me start this day praising you.
I often pray for strength and good judgment
    and other graces to get me through the day.
This morning I'd simply like to sing your praises.
Let me not focus on my weakness or my needs.
Rather, let me tell you that I love you
    and appreciate your great love for me.
You are my loving God,
    the giver of all good gifts.
    the source of all goodness.
Lord, you are my happiness and my destiny.
I depend upon you for my every breath.
May all my waking hours glorify you. Amen.

Overly Serious

Good morning, Lord.
Many of us are affected with the disease
    of being too serious.
Inside we are locked in grim determination,
    convinced there will be no success
    if we slacken our earnest efforts.
    It is a seriousness we entertain
    because we feel it's the only way
    for responsible people to act.
We think we need a no-nonsense attitude
    or else there will be little fulfillment in life.
Help us to be aware of your grace and love, Lord.
We overly serious people
    need to place greater trust in you. Amen.

May 27

Graceful Loser

Good morning, Lord.

Help me to be graceful in losing.

Of course, I want to be a winner.

Certainly, I must strive for the first prize,
    the golf championship, the academic medal.

But no one can win in all competitions.

Give me the grace to rejoice in another's good fortune,
    to be enthusiastic in congratulations.

Stamping my feet, wringing my hands is juvenile.

There is more respect for those who do not win
    when they give their best in the contest.

And there are no losers in your sight, Lord.

You see the sincerity in our hearts.

Thank you, Lord, for this perspective Amen.

May 28

Repentance

Good morning, Lord.

There is a masquerade that leads to misery;
    it has an old-fashioned name of sin.

Yes, there is sin, and I am a sinner.

I'm glad I said it; it relieves me.

It is good for me to admit
    my willful infractions of your holy will.

That is a step on the way back to you.

You love me despite my sins,
    but you expect me to repent.

The devil, the father of lies,
    whispers there is happiness in sin.

I have fallen for that all too often.

Give me strength to do your will, Lord. Amen.

Sincerity

Good morning, Lord.
I pray for the grace to live out
    what I believe in my heart.
When I find myself struggling at times,
    help me to be true to myself
    and above all to you.
Once I become convinced of the right move,
    may I have the courage to take the step.
May genuine concern for others guide me.
May I keep in mind the wisdom
    of your sacred commandments.
Thy will be done, Lord, not mine.
Guide me along the road to prudence.
May I praise you by the sincerity of my life. Amen.

Stumbling

Good morning, Lord.
Everyone stumbles now and then.
When we do, it's good to laugh at ourselves,
    get up, and get on with living.
Some people are so preoccupied with mistakes,
    anchored mentally in the errors of their judgment.
It need not even have been their fault.
Those who profit by their mistakes
    turn their mis-experiences around.
This becomes a step in the process of maturing.
Positive thinking makes the difference—
    and trust in you, Lord.
You have enough love and strength for us all.
Teach me to make the best of the worst. Amen.

Seeing

Good morning, Lord.

"That I may see" is a prayer for all of us.

Sight is a blessing seldom thought of—
    until threatened.

But many of us with sight fail to see.

We walk through the day
    unaware of the blessings around us.

Some are blind to the beauty in others,
    the kindnesses we receive,
        the thoughtful gestures of caring people.

Sharpen our powers of observation, Lord,
    to be aware of the poor, the lonely, the sensitive.

May we recognize our chances to serve others.

Whatever we do to others,
    we do to you. Amen.

Gracious Receiver

Good morning, Lord.
Help me to be a gracious receiver.
There are generous people who want
    to show their love, share their blessings
    on birthdays and anniversaries,
    or for no special reason at all.
They show their feelings by giving gifts.
A child may pluck a colorful weed
    and present it to his mother,
    or carry home a masterpiece from art class.
I know it's more blessed to give than receive,
    but there is also a graciousness in receiving.
Help me to be fittingly appreciative,
    especially of your graces, Lord. Amen.

Busy World

Good morning, Lord.
Is it possible to find you in a busy world?
At times we are so preoccupied
    with work, meals, play, and travel.
Looking upon us all on Earth,
    do you smile at our pace, our searching,
    our unnecessary trips, our frenzied efforts?
And the noise—sounds of construction,
    big machines roaring, snarling traffic,
    stereos and TVs blasting through open windows.
Do we crowd you out of our lives?
Do we drown out your voice?
Let us not lose touch with you, Lord.
May we walk with you this day. Amen.

Sharing

Good morning, Lord.
Can we not do more for people in the "third world"?
Their plight is portrayed in newspapers and on TV.
We daily witness the wars, diseases, and floods;
    swollen bellies and blank stares reveal
    the stark famine of countless children.
Millions in barrios are trapped in the depths
    of seemingly insurmountable poverty.
Sensitize our consciousness.
Fire us with love and zeal for them, Lord.
The practical love we express for them
    you accept as done for yourself:
"Whatsoever you do for the least . . ."
Thank you for your blessings and the desire to share.
Amen.

Challenges

Good morning, Lord.
We become discouraged for many reasons,
    but are any of them really good?
There are many reasons
    why we should not become demoralized,
    but we seem to forget them when the pressure is on.
We are always in your presence, Lord.
Nothing happens without your knowledge.
Your love for us is overwhelming.
Our misfortunes are but challenges,
    occasions for us to mature, to glorify you.
Inspire us all with courage this morning.
The spirit is willing but the flesh all too weak.
Thank you for your strength. Amen.

Heart Made of Gold

Good morning, Lord.
I know a person with many friends.
He makes people feel good, happy to know him.
He is not handsome or wealthy,
    but his heart is in the right place
    and it is made of gold.
Thank you for generous men and women
    whose pleasant dispositions are contagious.
May their good qualities rub off on me.
Help me to appreciate such friends,
    and to emulate their generosity and concern,
    their cheerfulness and modesty.
Such wonderful people are clearly a blessing.
It is only right to commend them to you. Amen.

A Loving Person

Good morning, Lord.
What should I do today to please you,
    to make your holy will known?
What can I do today
    to fulfill my purpose in life?
Give alms? Visit the lonely?
Do an honest day's work?
I am determined to be a good person,
    to be the person you want me to be.
How do I express my love for you, Lord,
    except by loving others?
Help me to recognize my opportunities:
    on the phone, at work, among family members.
May I give you glory by loving others. Amen.

June 7
Street Person
Good morning, Lord.
I passed a man without speaking to him.
He was obviously one of those anonymous
    people without a permanent residence.
If I had greeted him cheerfully,
    would he have reacted angrily,
    telling me to mind my own business?
Was he deep in thought,
    or just lonely or downhearted, as he appeared?
I pray for him now, that you will bless him,
    and I pray you pardon me for not saying hello.
A friendly greeting is inexpensive and easy to do;
    it might have made his day.
Give me the courage to reach out. Amen.

June 8
Faith
Good morning, Lord.
I'm inspired when I witness the faith of others,
    men and women who face grim realities
    with confidence, saying, "God will provide."
Their testimony does something for me.
I am reminded of the power of faith,
    how it sustains us, adds depth to my life.
Without faith in you, Lord,
    life lacks the most important of all dimensions.
How good to have the example of faithful people.
They pray together,
    praising you in good times and bad.
They pray for one another, providing mutual support.
Thank you, Lord, for those of faith
    who show us their deep convictions. Amen.

Recharging Batteries

Good morning, Lord.
"I gets weary . . . tired of living . . ."
These lyrics catch up sentiments
   we all feel from time to time.
We just seem to go on and on;
   "we just keep rolling along."
Give us the common sense, Lord,
   to rest, to put our feet up and take it easy.
The human body and spirit deserve relaxation.
Too many "rush orders," daily deadlines.
Prayerful people, meditative men and women,
   discover ways to recharge their batteries.
May we come to trust you a little more, Lord,
   and rely a little less on ourselves. Amen.

Monotony

Good morning, Lord.
Help us who struggle with job monotony.
We often do the same labor,
   repeating old patterns and routines.
Let us experience satisfaction
   in realizing the good we accomplish.
No one is individually sufficient in our world;
   one field of labor complements another.
We need each other, support one another.
Skills come to perfection through repetition.
Inspire us to look beyond the present task
   to the finished product,
     to the services we render each other.
Inspire our creative talents and imaginations. Amen.

June 11
Contrary Moods
Good morning, Lord.
I'm in one of those moods: sluggish!
I can't seem to get started today.
Sometimes I wake up refreshed,
     eager to move, to engage in the day's challenges.
Today? The blahs!
Something in the body chemistry.
Strange how the spirit is modified by the body.
Only you understand us perfectly, Lord.
I offer you my day with its sluggish start.
See beyond this mood to the sincerity of my life.
Help me to overcome the present inertia.
Bless all who persevere in loving you,
     despite contrary moods. Amen.

June 12
Sunrise
Good morning, Lord.
Sunrise is often the best time of the day.
It is quiet; it is peaceful.
The wheels of activity aren't fully in gear.
It is an ideal time to listen.
I am inclined to listen for your word,
     to praise you for the beauty of the moment.
Fill my heart, Lord, with your grace.
Teach me your ways, your thoughts.
Guide me with your wisdom.
Let me approach the day's challenges confidently,
     without fear, without anxiety.
May the tranquility of this moment linger.
Thank you for this and for your love. Amen.

Frustrations

Good morning, Lord.
Help me to manage my frustrations today.
They exist in everyone's life.
Some of us handle them better than others.
Many have tempers and often explode.
Others smolder on the inside.
What, after all, is frustration
    but not having our own way on cue?
It is discovering we met a deadline today
    when the order was due yesterday.
Give us strength, Lord, and patience
    and the grace "to stay loose."
The stress of being uptight would go away
    if we would look at the big picture. Amen.

Growing Old

Good morning, Lord.
Look with favor on all who feel
    they're growing old, reaching life's twilight.
Some try to conceal it; they are forever "thirty."
Some attempt to camouflage the years,
    covering them with cosmetics.
Some men and women mature gracefully,
    facing reality and the calendar
    with a shrug, a grin, and a chuckle.
Help us all to live up to our potential,
    to ignore society's arbitrary retirement age.
May all who have advanced in wisdom and age
    and experience and expertise
    flourish in their ageless prime. Amen.

June 15

All for God

Good morning, Lord.
I offer you my day:
    my thoughts, my words, my actions.
I offer them knowing
    that you can do without them nicely.
The world is yours, Lord;
    you create all; you command all.
But you also appreciate gestures of generosity.
Offering my day is like saying
    I wish it all to be according to your holy will.
May all that I do show my love for you.
I came into this world with nothing
    and shall leave with nothing.
Please accept the gift of myself. Amen.

June 16

The Sick

Good morning, Lord.
Brighten the day for all hospital patients.
Bring cheer and consolation to those
    confined in convalescent centers and at home.
Fill them with grace and strength
    and courage and spirit.
From the darkness of their negative thoughts
    enkindle the spark of their hope.
Each must trust in you, Lord.
Each must come to a conviction of your love.
You know their sickness and affliction,
    however long, intense, or bewildering.
Bless all these people
    in their physical or mental illnesses. Amen.

People in Pain

Good morning, Lord.
In the peace and comfort of this early hour
    I am conscious of those in pain.
I hear them groan in their anguish.
Be kind to all who are suffering;
    speed their relief and remedy.
Physical, emotional, and mental distress
    have always been with us,
    and continually challenge us.
I know, Lord, that you wish us no harm.
Transform this evil into spiritual good.
Give heart to all who love you,
    especially those confounded
    by this mystery of your holy will. Amen.

Morning Peace

Good morning, Lord.
This first cup of coffee is a morning ritual.
I'm the only one up at the moment.
My brain is yet not weary from the day's details.
It's just you and me and quiet conversation.
I enjoy these peaceful, unhurried moments,
    inviting you into my life.
People call it prayer time or meditation.
It is a special sharing and I am so blessed.
My thoughts come together;
    solutions seem to emerge.
Other problems persist,
    but, together, we can reduce them to size.
Lord, it's nice being with you. Amen.

June 19
One Step at a Time
Good morning, Lord.
There's no other way to meet the day's challenges
    except to begin.
Sometimes they come at me all at once.
There's too much to do and not enough hours.
Lumped together, my responsibilities
    rise before me like a mountain.
Then I start putting one foot in front of the other.
I keep my eyes fixed on the goal ahead.
Over time, steadily, there is progress.
I have to re-educate myself daily
    about taking one step at a time.
And about remembering I am not alone.
Thank you, Lord, for your presence. Amen.

June 20
Are You Listening?
Good morning, Lord.
I have been thinking lately about people
    who wonder if you hear their prayers.
Parents do not always listen to their children,
    husbands their wives, or teachers their pupils,
    and vice versa, of course.
We turn each other off like radios or TVs.
But it is different with you, Lord.
You have our best interests at heart.
We are always in your caring providence.
We think you listen as we do;
    how grossly inappropriate that would be.
Thank you, gracious Lord, for listening,
    for answering prayers the best way possible. Amen.

Family Life

Good morning, Lord.
Family life is vital for our nation's health.
Bless mothers and fathers, sons and daughters.
May all homes be havens of happiness,
 places where family members love one another,
 showing their concern by loving courtesies.
Inspire novelists, playwrights, all authors
 to write about lives that encourage
 harmony and respect in the family.
May children experience their home life
 as loving, serene, and very happy.
Lord, you are the unseen guest
 in every home, at every table.
May all families recognize your presence. Amen.

God's Pleasure

Good morning, Lord.
What is your pleasure today?
Now that's a change in approach.
I usually have dozens of projects
 that I present to you for your blessing.
You are familiar with my prayers and desires,
 but tell me what I can do for you.
You do not need me, but let me serve you.
Tell me what is closest to your holy will.
A willingness to say "Thy will be done"
 is an improvement, a step in the right direction.
Many people want to know your holy will.
They want to return to church,
 to a reformed life, to peaceful consciences.
Bless us with a desire to do your will. Amen.

June 23
Self-Centered Prayer
Good morning, Lord.
I wonder, Do I pray for the right intentions?
I know I'm free to pray for what I want,
    but do I petition you for trivial things?
My personal conveniences?
When so many people are suffering—
    earthquakes and famines,
    wars and bankruptcies,
    leaving them in devastated condition—
    I must get out of my self-centeredness.
So I pray for all my brothers and sisters now.
Help them in their great needs.
I know that you love us all tremendously.
Thank you for answering this prayer. Amen.

June 24
Standing Firm
Good morning, Lord.
I realize that nothing is correct
    unless it follows your holy will.
"Thy will be done" is an essential condition.
Happiness is knowing your will
    and having the courage to do it.
But this explains my frequent discontent:
    I may pit my will against that of others.
Enlighten me, Lord, to learn
    when to stand firm, when to challenge,
    and when to concede there is a better way.
Guide me in my thinking;
    inspire me to be open-minded and humble.
Thank you for this grace. Amen.

God's Day

Good morning, Lord.
This day is yours, not mine.
I offer you all I do and think.
I pray that my day is not for personal gain,
    but opportunities to praise your holy name.
You have blessed me with life,
    with faith and with the promise of paradise.
You have loved me from the womb.
This is your world.
Strengthen my resolve;
    enlighten my understanding;
    accept my humble offering.
I pray I might live up to your expectations.
Thank you for life's challenges and rewards. Amen.

Staying Loose

Good morning, Lord.
I woke today less troubled than yesterday.
The weight on my shoulders
    lessened overnight.
This happens frequently.
Prayer and a good night's sleep keep me going.
It's related to my disposition,
    how I give and take during the day.
An athlete performs well when relaxed.
Me, too.
I'm like a violin string stretched beyond pitch
    making miserable sounds.
I place myself in your hands, Lord.
Together we will succeed. Amen.

June 27
Praying and Believing
Good morning, Lord.
I have been praying to you for a long time:
   in the dead of night after a nightmare,
   at high noon, in public and in private,
   to praise, to petition, to ask for pardon.
I always feel better after prayer
because I know you always listen to me.
Over the years our conversation has improved.
I think I have become more understanding,
   more confident in you, Lord,
   and I am learning to listen.
I can express myself and this helps a great deal.
I realize that prayer habits must develop,
   and that above all I must believe and trust. Amen.

June 28
Second Chances
Good morning, Lord.
Once we have made a serious mistake,
   we have to battle back from despair and guilt.
It is a psychological cloud
   that seems to follow us everywhere.
No one is without error or sin.
Send grace and peace to the repentant, Lord.
Let the heavily burdened know
   that forgiveness is only a prayer away.
You do not wish anyone to be frozen,
   petrified, in a self-deprecating state.
Let the gloom give way to bright sunshine.
Your goodness and mercy allow second chances.
How fortunate for me and for everyone. Amen.

Personal Peace

Good morning, Lord.

I seek the peace that only you can give.

There is no escape from my responsibilities.

Today I face a continuation of yesterday's details.

Challenges to anger and frustration will come.

How do some people manage to smile
    and maintain such exterior calm?

What do the tranquil know that I don't?

That elusive disposition of mind and heart?

Resignation to your holy will?

Clear conscience? Knowing when to be satisfied?

Let me walk with you, Lord,
    and get my own act together.

Thank you for this new and wonderful day. Amen.

Dying

Good morning, Lord.

I'd like to talk with you about dying.

It isn't anything I'm in a hurry to do.

In fact, I'm like those who figure it happens to others.

My own encounter is in the dim, distant future.

Will I really have to give an account of my life?

Small wonder I'm not in a rush.

No way I can make up for all the mistakes.

Most of the violations were years ago
    before I developed some common sense.

Since I can't make restitution for all my sins,
    I'll really have to trust in your great mercy.

Of course, there is still time to do good,
    and to recall that perfect love knows no fear. Amen.

Cheerfulness

Good morning, Lord.
I pray for all the cheerful people
   who brighten my days,
     whose are so patient they don't show the strain,
     whose graciousness is a charm so warm
     that it melts the coldest hearts.
These are the popular folks
   who are generous and loving,
   perpetually hopeful that all incidents,
   all stories will have happy endings.
Send more of these beautiful souls into my life.
Favor us with your grace
   that I may be equally cheerful and optimistic.
Your blessing, Lord, on cheerful people. Amen.

Questions

Good morning, Lord.
Some days I'm full of questions.
A bumper sticker says, "Sailors have more fun."
So I ask myself, "Doing what"?
Or, "More fun than whom"?
What would we do without questions
   to drive knowledge forward,
   or to entertain ourselves?
Then there are the eternal questions:
   about life, truth, beauty, human destiny.
Thank you, Lord, for the answers we have,
and for the desire to find even more.
And thank you for telling us that you are
   "the way, the truth, and the life." Amen.

July 3

Birds

Good morning, Lord.
Why do birds "sing"?
There are sweet sounds, musical tweets,
    and there are sour ones, scraping the eardrum.
A seagull croaks up a storm if another steals its food.
Canaries light up our lives,
    tripping the scale with a light touch.
Most of us take these friends for granted.
We notice the robins in the spring;
    we observe geese flying south in the fall.
Help us to appreciate the role of birds
    in the environment's delicate balance,
May we respect them always,
    and be grateful for the gift they are. Amen.

July 4

Serious Illness

Good morning, Lord.
We pray for those with serious illness.
Their future uncertain, they know fear and anxiety.
How will we react if we become seriously ill?
Sadness and depression alone solve nothing.
We need to be resigned to your holy will.
We need to make sincere resolutions
    to lead better lives if and when we recover.
If our condition is irreversible,
    we must make adjustments for the present,
    and for eternity.
"Do not be afraid," you tell us.
You love us and make all things turn out for good.
Grace with your presence those who are ill. Amen.

Hope

Good morning, Lord.
Hope is a small word with enormous promise.
We undertake nothing without it.
Inspire the weary, those who find life burdensome.
Light up the lives of those
who see only darkness ahead.
The unemployed who feel rejected,
the discouraged and the lonely,
the homeless and the hungry—
fill them all with hope.
Where there is creativity and enterprise,
there is still hope.
You, Lord, are our hope.
Fill our hearts with this comfort. Amen.

Positive Thinking

Good morning, Lord.
Bless me with positive thinking this day.
Nothing will happen today
that together we cannot handle.
I have friends ready to help and comfort me,
and experts ready to counsel me.
No door is closed so tightly
that it cannot be opened.
Every challenge can be met.
I rely on you, Lord;
you are why I can be upbeat this day.
You allow me to be tried at times,
only to bring out the best in me.
Thank you for all your graces this day. Amen.

Appreciation

Good morning, Lord.
Some people are good about expressing thanks.
They write, they phone, they are so appreciative.
Their appreciation inspires me.
I know you have been good to me;
    your love continues to touch me.
Every day is an occasion to thank you, Lord.
I can never adequately express my appreciation.
All the carefully composed thank-you notes
    hardly describe your love for me.
How true the lyrics of the old song:
    "You'll never know just how much I love you."
As I encounter your signs of love today,
    I'll think about the gratitude I owe you. Amen.

Cover-Ups

Good morning, Lord.
I do many things to justify myself.
Who hasn't engaged in cover-ups?
But nothing can set me free—except the truth.
I have to be honest with myself.
Self-deception only compounds my original mistake.
I know I have attempted to justify my sins:
    "The others are doing it, too."
    "I'm not as bad as my neighbor."
    "I could have done a lot worse."
Hollow phrases, Lord, insisting on my own will.
Sometimes I rationalize with myself,
    justifying that I was correct all along.
Forgive me, Lord, for this gross dishonesty. Amen.

Cherished Moments

Good morning, Lord.
Quiet places are at a premium these days.
This is a busy world, and a noisy one.
It's so good to have a few minutes with you.
I can kneel in the cool repose of a church,
    recline beneath a tree,
    or find peaceful solitude in my room.
How much I need your assurance.
It comes to me in prayer, in unhurried conversation.
Time with you refreshes my soul.
You are the source of my inner strength.
As this day picks up in pace, gains momentum,
    help me to reflect how near you are.
Thank you for these cherished moments. Amen.

New Day

Good morning, Lord.
A new day brings new hope, new blessings.
There are songs to sing, places to go, people to visit.
We can take the time to help friends in need,
    to reach out to the lonely,
    to cheer those saddened by tragedy and loss.
This is a new day to begin new adventures.
Thank you, Lord, for the grace to recognize
    the awesome potential of these waking hours.
Let me not think today will merely be
    a dull, routine, carbon copy of yesterday.
You have given me new life
    and life is what I make it.
For all today's blessings, thank you. Amen.

July 11
Same Old Prayers

Good morning, Lord.
How many times have you heard the same prayers,
    as parents the same questions of their children,
    as teachers the same inquiries of their students?
We think our ideas are so original,
    so characteristic of ourselves.
Your children worldwide pray to you, Lord.
Still, nothing is boring, repetitious,
    or too insignificant, when we speak to you.
It is because you see our hearts,
    and we have your undivided attention.
It is because you are our God
    and love us with an overwhelming love.
Praise, honor, and glory, Lord! Amen.

July 12
Turning to God

Good morning, Lord.
Can I start this day telling you my troubles?
Sometimes I feel ill at ease, disquieted,
    unsure of myself, I guess.
Can it be body chemistry?
Anyway, talking to you restores my confidence.
My uneasiness may be normal,
    to be expected from time to time.
You allow this only for my greater good,
    to make me aware of my frailty, my humanity.
These feelings dispel that old presumption:
    "I can do or control everything by myself."
I know what I need, where to turn, Lord:
    to you. Amen.

Near at Hand

Good morning, Lord.
Some people act as if you don't hear them.
Some perceive you as distant and uncaring,
    a god who remains coldly aloof.
This is not the way it is, of course.
You care for each one of us.
You have concerned yourself with our welfare;
    you have involved yourself with our daily affairs.
Nothing escapes your loving concern.
I wouldn't want my friends
    to think I am indifferent to their pleas.
You have revealed your merciful kindness.
Help me to see the events in my life
    in the light of your goodness, Lord. Amen.

Unique Day

Good morning, Lord.
This is a day to rejoice in;
    there will be no other day like it.
It will bring new opportunity to praise you,
    it will bring me a little closer to you.
Inspire me to be imaginative this day.
Let me recognize its unique blessings.
I have my responsibilities and routines,
    but let me see my friends, family, job
    with new eyes and fresh appreciation
    for its opportunities and challenges.
There is nothing to hinder my progress today.
It is to be lived with joy,
    making the most of all I have. Amen.

July 15
Feeling Lonely

Good morning, Lord.
I feel very lonely, I have to admit.
Not all the time, of course.
I'm frequently in contact with others,
    and we talk about the weather and other things.
There are kind and thoughtful gestures,
    business deals, phone calls, errands.
I go from one busy moment to the next.
Then why do I still feel alone?
Probably I don't reach out enough;
    I don't give enough of myself.
Loneliness may disappear doing deeds for others,
    sharing a little bit of our love.
Thank you, Lord, even for my loneliness. Amen.

July 16
Praying

Good morning, Lord.
You and I have been talking for a long time,
    years and years, a few minutes each day.
We never seem to run out of conversation.
Sometimes I just sit and listen,
    waiting in silence for you to speak to my heart.
And I also tell you my concerns and feelings.
Such quiet times are good, a chance to reflect.
Often I seek your will in prayer.
I cannot go wrong when I do that.
Trying to discern your will makes up
    a good part of our communication.
How can it be otherwise?
Thank you, Lord, for helping me to pray. Amen.

God-With-Us

Good morning, Lord.
Your love for us surpasses our hopes and desires.
How different our lives would be
    if we really grasped this overriding fact.
Often we picture our relationship this way:
    we are here, you are there;
    we call for help, pardon, favors.
There is remoteness, desperation in such prayer.
There is no need for this mentality.
You are near. You are love.
You are God-with-us.
How pleasing it must be to you
    when we relax in your presence,
    stop reaching, and simply bask in your love. Amen.

New Realities

Good morning, Lord.
Fill my mind with new light and understanding.
I can just repeat my yesterdays,
    run off carbon copies of words and deeds,
    carry off the same routine—except for your grace.
Every day is a brand new adventure.
    meeting new friends, learning new facts,
    experiencing new realities.
There is so much to discover,
    and the challenges are limitless.
Your world holds endless fascination;
    let me approach it with new eyes and new mind.
And all of this wonderful world is nothing
    in comparison with you, Lord. Amen.

July 19
Busy About Many Things
Good morning, Lord.
We'll shortly be busy about many things:
   washing, dressing, praying,
   breakfasting, commuting, working,
   all doing "our own thing."
Yesterday's pursuits are resumed.
I pray for great serenity within myself, Lord,
   control over my anxieties.
Can I do this in a feverish society?
I think so.
I have to keep a clear head,
   take things in stride, with confidence in you.
I have to remind myself
   of your presence and your love. Amen.

July 20
No More Delay
Good morning, Lord.
I start this day with strong intentions.
You've heard this before, haven't you?
No more putting off details until later.
No more procrastination.
There's been enough delay in my life.
I especially want to get my interior life in order,
   so please forgive all my sins.
I regret them deeply, Lord.
I depend on your goodness and mercy.
Then with your peace in my heart
   I'll do my best to make all things right.
I'll bet there are a lot of people like me.
Thank you for your patience, Lord. Amen.

Sleepless

Good morning, Lord.
Sometimes I can't sleep. Nighthawk, they say.
Every now and then there is a real sleepless night,
    waking up after a couple hours
    and unable to drowse off again.
All-night radio helps: talk shows,
    24-hour news, music, commercials.
Look what sound sleepers are missing.
The wee hours are good praying hours, Lord.
You and I talk quite a bit.
Used to be I'd try so hard
    to sleep and get so frustrated.
Now I thank you for the distress.
I offer it up. Less hassle. More peace. Amen.

On My Way

Good morning, Lord.
When you call me, when it's my turn to die,
    the important things in life
    will no longer be important.
I know it will be "one of these days"
    when I'm driving along, or napping, or jogging.
Who knows besides you, Lord?
The prospect of death doesn't make me
    indifferent about my work or people.
People may say, "What's the difference?
Don't get involved. Don't get attached.
You're going to leave it all anyway."
Everyone and everything in this life is important.
I'm here now, but relentlessly I'm on my way. Amen.

July 23

God Is Near

Good morning, Lord.
The Bible reminds us how near you are:
"God is our refuge and strength,
    a helper close at hand, in time of distress . . ."
There is never a need to shout to you, Lord.
You are present, ever attentive to our pleas.
As parents look lovingly at their children,
    so do you regard each of us.
You wait for us to respond to your love.
You tell us that if we ask we shall receive,
    if we seek we shall find.
It pleases you to hear our prayers,
    which is one way that you stand with us.
May I be mindful of your presence this day. Amen.

July 24

Unshakable Trust

Good morning, Lord.
I trust in you and refuse to be shaken.
I am nothing without trust in you.
What else is there to depend on?
I have no reason not to trust you,
    my rock and my refuge.
When all else fails, you do not disappoint me.
Bridges may collapse and castles crumble.
Businesses go bankrupt and friends pass away,
    but you, Lord, are always at my side,
    "as constant as the northern star."
I used to think I was self-sufficient.
How good it is to rely on only you absolutely!
Let me never again ignore your presence. Amen.

Being Merciful

Good morning, Lord.
It is written, "Blessed are the merciful,
for they shall obtain mercy."
I need to remember that
when I get all steamed up, vocal and righteous,
I'm like a lot of people, blaming others,
criticizing, shouting my indignation at others.
Who made me the judge, anyway?
I lash out and editorialize with the greatest of ease.
Let me always be thoughtful and forgiving.
and think about casting the first stone.
Mercy—forgiveness—is a divine prerogative.
Mischief-makers, the criminal, and the petty
can experience your mercy—and mine. Amen.

Pure Praise

Good morning, Lord.
I'm not asking for anything special today.
Usually I pray for graces and favors.
I really do need to be sustained daily.
I am continually in your presence.
Your providence envelops the universe.
Perhaps, I tell myself, it's good not to be
constantly petitioning for this blessing or that.
Let me recognize and acknowledge you for yourself—
all loving, caring, compassionate, forgiving.
This is a moment to meditate on your goodness,
to savor your sweet presence and undying love.
I praise and glorify you, Lord.
I'm sorry for not expressing this more often. Amen.

July 27
Pacing Yourself
Good morning, Lord.
Sometimes I crowd too much into a limited space,
    trying to accomplish more
    than is reasonable in a normal day.
I pressure myself into believing that will power
    and honest effort can get the job done.
And sometimes I'm right;
    we do pamper ourselves at times.
Positive thinking, planning, and diligence get results,
    but working too hard and too long takes its toll.
There is value in timing, pacing yourself.
We do better work when relaxed;
    the creative thoughts flow more freely.
Give me balance and perspective, Lord. Amen.

July 28
Admitting Mystery
Good morning, Lord.
I admit to mysteries.
There are matters I do not comprehend
    because they are simply beyond me.
I recognize that your knowledge surpasses all.
You give me the ability to know truth,
    but not to encompass all truth.
My mind constantly searches,
    thirsting to drink from the font of understanding.
I seek you, Lord, who are truth itself.
As I mature, teach me to be humble in this pursuit.
Knowledge for its own sake is not the end.
Grant me, instead, the peace
    that surpasses all understanding. Amen.

Different Drummer

Good morning, Lord.
Let me recognize goodness wherever it exists.
Prejudice blinds me and clouds my thinking.
I withhold praise when certain people do good deeds.
Acclaiming their actions may be taken to mean
    I approve the persons performing them.
Sincere men and women walk your paths,
    even if they are "different" than I am.
They march to the beat of a different drummer.
How pleasing it is for you, Lord,
    to receive glory and honor from all people.
You look to the heart of your sons and daughters.
Inspire me to acknowledge truth and beauty,
    wherever they may be found. Amen.

Free From Distraction

Good morning, Lord.
Let me listen to you speak to my heart.
I am filled with sights and sounds.
Television and radio provide a kaleidoscope
    of music, conversation, commercials, weather.
The morning paper reports its variety
    of political, civic, social, and economic events.
I speak with family, neighbors, and friends
    about health, wealth, and whatnot.
How marvelously the brain sorts it all out
    and makes sense of all these bids for attention.
But I need quiet moments, Lord,
    to say "Our Father, who art in heaven."
May I hear your voice free from distraction. Amen.

July 31
Harmony of Wills
Good morning, Lord.
Nothing really matters except what you want.
Your will is all-powerful,
    but you have made us with wills of our own.
They may be exercised freely
    only to give you the glory you deserve.
When we pray "Thy will be done,"
    we ask that our decisions be pleasing to you.
It means that we want our individual wills
    to be in harmony with yours.
We are rebellious at times, acting defiantly,
    grasping at forbidden fruits.
May we be meek and humble, Lord,
    walking your ways, doing your deeds. Amen.

Vacation

Good morning, Lord.
Many people are on vacation,
    having taken to the highways, the lakes,
    the camping grounds, the picnic areas.
Some fly to faraway places, to exclusive beaches,
    to highrise hotels and mountain resorts.
But they are never far from you, Lord,
    for this is your world, wherever they go.
Nothing is hidden from your sight
    nor from your loving concern.
In their search for diversion and relaxation,
    may they refresh their souls, revive their spirits,
    and be strengthened in faith
    and come closer to you. Amen.

Continued Favor

Good morning, Lord.
Praise and honor to you this day.
Thank you for another opportunity to serve you.
Fill my mind with positive thoughts.
Let me act with the loving assurance
    that you are at my side,
    you who are Lord, God-with-us.
Each day I must be reminded of this
    and feel the impact of your grace.
The remembrance of my weakness, your strength
    is what I need to live my life in your sight
    and meet all challenges confidently.
You are my loving Father.
I pray for your continued favor. Amen.

August 3
Everyday People
Good morning, Lord.
Every day I encounter many people:
  the supermarket cashier, the mail deliverer,
  the gas station attendant, the meter reader—
  all wonderful people, people you love.
I react to them according to my mood:
  bright and cheerful at one time,
  but abrupt and grumpy at another.
Help me to have a genuine appreciation
  of every boy and girl, man and woman.
Let me discover how lovable they are—
  in and of themselves,
  and not based on my mood.
Help me, Lord, to love everyone. Amen.

August 4
Easy Talk
Good morning, Lord.
It gets easier talking to you each day.
Praying is not meant to be a chore.
Who really minds chatting with someone
  who is loving and understanding?
Like a good habit, praying becomes easier
  when it's done every day,
  even if it's only for a moment.
We feel clumsy and ill at ease with strangers,
  especially if we seldom converse.
You, Lord, are never meant to be a stranger.
Still it does happen that the very busy
  don't quite get around to honoring you in prayer.
I thank you, Lord, for your great patience. Amen.

Expressing Thanks

Good morning, Lord.
It is not difficult to thank you for blessings.
I know it pleases you when I am grateful.
I could thank you every moment of the day
    without ever adequately expressing the thanks
    your love and generosity deserve.
Everything we are, everything we have
    is a gift, an expression of your bountiful love.
I see colorful flowers and explosive sunsets
    and I thank you for sight.
I listen to sweet melodies, enchanting music
    and I thank you for hearing.
I feel my heart beat and perceive my breathing
    and I thank you for life. Amen.

Faith and Presence

Good morning, Lord.
This is the beginning of a new day.
There is nothing you and I cannot manage.
How reassuring to know you are with me!
People of faith do not walk alone.
They are deeply aware of your presence.
You invite our absolute confidence.
I am at times fearful or anxious,
    but I take heart knowing you are at my side.
You are my strength; your grace is sufficient.
The greater my faith and trust in you,
    the more peaceful I remain.
This is going to be a good day.
Your presence casts out my anxiety. Amen.

Last Day

Good morning, Lord.
Now and then I pretend it's the last day of my life.
Who knows? Perhaps it is.
What does a person do with those last 24 hours?
I think I should smile a lot. Why not?
The great commandment is to love you, Lord,
    totally, with my whole heart and soul.
And I should love everyone around me.
If love is what my life is all about,
    why should I not spend this last day smiling,
    knowing you have graced me with a life of love?
There is really no excuse for not loving.
This is the first day in the rest of my life,
    whether or not it turns out to be my last. Amen.

August 8
Morning Offering

Good morning, Lord.
I offer you my day, such as it will be.
I know it is not a spectacular gift.
I probably won't do anything
    extraordinary, heroic for you today.
Accept this offering as a gesture of love.
May my thoughts, words, and deeds be pleasing.
My heart is in the right place; my intentions good.
Let me overcome temptation
    and be prudent in fulfilling your will.
Let me not compromise your commandments.
I am aware of my faults and weaknesses,
    but I want this to be a day dedicated to pleasing you.
This is my conscious resolve. Amen.

Prayer Time

Good morning, Lord.
This is the best time of the day, the early hours.
Many now asleep will soon be stirring,
    dashing about, making breakfast,
    driving to work, getting ready for school.
This is my time to talk to you
    without telephones or doorbells.
Speak to me, Lord, in the peace of my heart.
Tell me how I may please you.
Let my priorities be your priorities.
Refine and purify my good intentions.
My life has sharper perspective after my prayer time.
You are always with me, only a prayer away,
    sustaining me with your love. Amen.

Looking Up

Good morning, Lord.
Give courage and strength to all
    whose spirits have plunged into despair.
Comfort the discouraged and sorrowing.
Let all see through the dark clouds
    and discover the silver lining of your love.
All of us are subject to trial and temptation.
We tell ourselves, "You're human and weak."
Do not allow us to indulge in self-pity.
Electrify our thinking. Renew our creativity.
Recharge every cell in our being.
We look down too easily, mired in our gloom.
Inspire us to look up to you, Lord,
    and to appreciate your divine presence. Amen.

Witness

Good morning, Lord.
I'm comforted by the faith of those around me.
The faith witness of friends and neighbors
    buoys up my spirit.
We do good for one another by our example.
When I witness someone patient in suffering,
    I realize how small I can be in my self-pity.
I try to be faithful because others show the way.
Faith in you, Lord, is reflected in their lives.
Good people make my life worth living.
I am sustained because friends and strangers
    are so dedicated and sincere of heart.
Keep my mind and soul open, Lord,
    to the positive influences around me. Amen.

Door to the Heart

Good morning, Lord.
You know that painting of you knocking
    at a door with no knob or handle.
Like the heart, it has to be opened from within.
Do I open my heart to those I meet?
I receive some more readily than others,
    warmer welcomes for those I love.
But do I exclude anyone from my life
    because he or she is poor or "different"?
Help me, Lord, to be basically kind to all I meet.
Let me not act superior or impolite
    with the sales clerk, immigrant, rubbish man—
    with any one of your children.
Let me be as receptive as you are with me. Amen.

Keeping in Touch

Good morning, Lord.
We pray not to be too busy
    and lose touch with you as the day goes on.
There is such a demand on our attention.
Even when people can take a moment for prayer,
    we see commuters absorbed in magazines.
Some are occupied with periodicals or documents,
    or work on lap-top computers.
This goes on from morning to night.
Then for many, it's television—
    news, sports, comedies, movies.
On the weekend they're too tired to go to church.
I hope we all make time for you, Lord,
    each day, sometime, somehow. Amen.

Magic Words

Good morning, Lord.
I'm upbeat at this early hour.
Somebody told me they love me.
There's nothing like a few words like that
    to make life seem so worthwhile.
This encourages me to communicate
    words of love to others.
If it does wonders for my spirits,
    it can do wonders for others.
Words like that—and God's words of love—
    can turn a day—a life—around.
I think I'll make a few phone calls
    and write a few letters today.
Lord, you're always telling me you love me. Amen.

August 15
God's Beauty

Good morning, Lord.
In our beautiful world
    there are sunrises and sunsets—
    and enough stunning scenery in between
    to satisfy our aesthetic hunger.
I'm taking time today to smell the flowers,
    to appreciate the hills and bees
    and blossoms and seas.
Beauty is in the eye of the beholder, they say.
But it isn't all relative and subjective.
I've got to believe you created beauty, Lord,
    making objects pleasing to sight and sound.
How blessed we are, Lord, to enjoy
    the wonderful work of your hands. Amen.

August 16
Being Loved

Good morning, Lord.
How pleasing it is to see children loved!
When showered with affection and care,
    they experience peace and contentment:
    no insecurity, no cause for anxiety.
And so it is with ourselves and you, Lord.
If we can say to ourselves, "God loves me,"
    interior peacefulness permeates our being.
We are your children.
You tell us "I love you" in a thousand ways.
Sharpen our appreciation of your love.
Your communication of it is unmistakable.
May we be receptive to it,
    and respond with our own love. Amen.

Small Talk with a Big God

Good morning, Lord.
I don't know what to say this morning.
I want to pray but the thoughts won't come.
So here I am as I am: sincere but speechless.
It isn't that I do not know how to pray.
It's just that I usually have specifics,
    but now I'm drawing blanks.
As husbands and wives sometimes experience,
    I may be all talked out
    or simply feel I have nothing to express.
Funny, isn't it? I'm chatting like mad
    about having nothing to say.
Small talk with a big God!
I know you are listening and love me. Amen.

Looking Outward

Good morning, Lord.
At times I'm confronted with the thought
    that I don't give enough attention to others.
My mind rattles about in endless concerns
    about myself, tied up in my own little world.
Talk about being trapped by my own consciousness!
How good it is to think of others.
To reach out is its own reward.
When I'm inspired to work selflessly for others,
    the comfort, the consolation is liberating.
I forget my troubles
    and expand my mind and heart,
    because my vision is outward
    to my brothers and sisters, Lord. Amen.

August 19
Divine Approval
Good morning, Lord.
I want your approval in all I do.
Nothing else really matters.
I cannot expect a pat on the back
 for every move I make.
Still, all of us look for affirmation,
 like children calling to parents to notice their feats.
I know I have your approval
 when I follow your holy will.
It's easy when the commandment is spelled out.
It's difficult in dilemmas
 and where there are few specifics.
You are pleased, Lord, with the sincere of heart.
Strengthen me in my personal convictions.
I thank you for the blessings this new day. Amen.

August 20
Wonderful World
Good morning, Lord.
Another new day in a wonderful world!
Everything I experience is a gift from you:
 the stars, Earth, the oceans and mountains,
 animals large and small, domestic and exotic,
 are all your handiwork.
And we humans, after your image and likeness,
 come in a variety of colors and cultures:
Chinese, Zulus, Chileans, Moroccans, Americans—
 all our brothers and sisters.
So much to appreciate, to be thankful for.
How is it, Lord, that we are so blessed,
 even to have you love us personally!
You overwhelm us with your graciousness. Amen.

The Glory of God
Good morning, Lord.
"Whether you eat or drink, whatever you do,
   you should do all for the glory of God."
All days should be a credit to you, our Creator.
If children delight in pleasing their parents,
   our pleasure should be in delighting you.
How can I please you this day?
You request nothing extraordinary or special.
Just the ordinary: thoughts, words, and deeds
   offered sincerely.
Little things are sanctifying
   because they are done with love
   and in response to your love.
Thank you, Lord, for loving me first. Amen.

Loving Is Everything
Good morning, Lord.
As I advance in wisdom and age,
   I am increasingly conscious of your love.
How can I respond, love you back?
The impact of these words
   gradually seeps into my mind:
   "What can I return to the Lord
   for all the Lord has done for me?"
I think perhaps I am getting somewhere
   in my relationship with you.
Loving is everything;
   generosity is the hallmark of true believers.
Selfishness and pettiness are the nothings.
Let me love everyone I meet today. Amen.

August 23
Lord's Delight
Good morning, Lord.
An old line can take on new meaning
　　almost as if we hadn't heard it before:
"The Lord takes delight in people,"
　　written centuries ago by the psalmist.
Your pleasure, Lord, is in us when we are loving.
It's possible to hold you at arm's length,
　　deal with you impersonally,
　　treat you as the distant, uninvolved supreme being.
That is not your way with us.
Your delight is in us, to be with us,
　　your children blessed with the life you give.
We are reassured when you are pleased with us.
May we know your holy will and do it. Amen.

August 24
Good for Evil
Good morning, Lord.
Let me always return good for evil.
For every harsh, insulting word,
　　let me speak patiently and kindly.
For every discourtesy and rude gesture,
　　let me be gracious and polite.
Let me undo the vicious cycle of violence.
"The meek will inherit the land."
Meekness is not weakness, but strength.
It's possible to oppose evil with nonviolence.
It is a matter of wisdom and prudence,
　　being bigger than the situation.
It is written, "A soft answer turns away wrath."
Help me to be loving, Lord. Amen.

Possessions

Good morning, Lord.
Advertising preaches values.
We praise products to sell them.
Cars, clothing, kitchen utensils, vacations—
    our happiness depends on them.
Help us to appreciate the good things in life,
    which we have through your generosity.
But give us discernment, the ability to distinguish.
Temper our burning desire for possessions.
Let them be so many means
    to helping the poor, sheltering the homeless,
    and clothing the destitute.
All things can be used for good,
    if our hearts are in the right place. Amen.

Another Day

Good morning, Lord.
How sweet to have another day to live!
Each day is a gift.
Sick people, those confronted with mortal danger,
    suddenly realize the blessing of carefree days.
Our days, like the hairs of our head, are numbered.
Days are for singing and playing.
Days are for caring and sharing.
Days are for loving and serving.
Days are for forgiving and being forgiven.
Days are for working and creating.
Days are for fresh efforts, for new starts.
Bless this new day.
Let it find us even closer to you, Lord. Amen.

August 27
Something Personal
Good morning, Lord.
If I were you, I would like someone
    to say something personal to me.
Prayers can be so formal at times.
When little children speak to me
    in their own inimitable, trusting way,
    I am really moved.
If we, your children, speak from the heart
    and mean the message for you alone,
      it's like an original Valentine or birthday card.
I love you, Lord, and I am happy I can say that.
How often have I pleaded for favors
I thought I could not live without.
I just want to praise you for yourself. Amen.

August 28
Finding Peace
Good morning, Lord.
Send your gift of peace to my troubled soul.
Peace to the restless, to the agitated and anxious.
Let me accept your peace;
    open my heart and let your sunlight in
    so that I might feel the warmth of your peace.
Help me to right all wrongs,
    to bring my sins to the surface and unburden
    the conscience of your prodigal child.
This confession is good for my soul.
It brings an interior calm,
    a feeling that I have been away, but now am back.
Everything will be all right again.
Let me experience the warmth of your embrace. Amen.

Uptight

Good morning, Lord.
How uptight I get at times.
So intent and anxious, I fail to smell the roses.
What is it, Lord? A fear of not succeeding?
Do I forget that you are around,
   that you understand, have a grasp on my situation?
With all my faith and trust,
   I still seem to revert to old attitudes,
   acting as if it all depended on me.
And who says what I am doing
   is so all-fired important, anyway?
Then I recall the lines about the lilies of the field,
   how they are under your loving care.
It's going to be a good day, Lord. Amen.

Personal Relationship

Good morning, Lord.
We have a little world of our own within us:
   our very private thoughts.
We share some of them, but not all.
We trust these precious thoughts
   to family and a few close friends.
They know us, understand us better.
And you, Lord, are the most trusted of all.
Welcome to my interior, personal world.
It is one thing to realize that you know them,
   even the deepest secrets of my heart.
It is still another to welcome you to them.
Many of us who claim faith in you
   often fail to establish a personal relationship. Amen.

Sooner Than That

Good morning, Lord.
I have a problem I don't know how to solve,
    something I discussed with you many times.
It refuses to go away.
Is this a blessing in disguise?
I renew my trust in you with each prayer.
Still, you are not to be rushed.
Of course, it involves the free will of another,
    and I know that you do not force one's will.
"Thy will be done, Lord."
St. Monica prayed for her son Augustine
    for 17 years
      before he had a change of heart.
Please help me sooner than that. Amen.

Too Little Time

Good morning, Lord.
It's good not to be rushed.
I'm always working against deadlines,
    so I appreciate the quiet, unpressured life.
We make more mistakes when we're in a hurry.
And we don't do well to rush our prayers either.
Some say they don't have time for church on Sunday.
You be the judge of that, Lord.
Too many people ration their conversation with you:
    too many things to do, too little time.
How good it is to have time
    to spend in your company, Lord.
Two or three minutes each day—uninterrupted—
    can keep me in touch with you. Amen.

Always Available

Good morning, Lord.
How comforting to believe in an all-loving God
    who is constantly accessible.
In times of temptation, you are there.
In times of joy, you are present.
There are bewildering, wrenching situations,
    but never are you distant.
In times of depression, you are with us.
Never do you withhold your grace, your self.
Do we turn to you more frequently in distress?
I suppose we do,
    but there is nothing like knowing you are with us.
How blest we are in our faith.
How empty our lives without you. Amen.

Faith

Good morning, Lord.
Bless those who sincerely seek you.
Many pray for the gift of faith, wishing to believe.
They struggle to embrace you, Lord,
  but their background is an obstacle:
    "No one ever taught me how to pray."
    "We never attended church."
    "Religion was not discussed. It seemed irrelevant."
The spiritually uninitiated sense an emptiness.
Believers possess an internal assurance they envy.
They feel a dimension missing from their lives.
Reward the sincerity of their hearts.
Let the good example and witness of your faithful
  lead them to you. Amen.

Pure of Heart

Good morning, Lord.
"Blessed are the pure of heart
  for they shall see God."
This formula for deep internal contentment—
  when one's main concern
  is not the correctness of external ritual
  but what is in the heart—
  is a condition for my relationship with you.
It keeps my vision focused on you, Lord.
We can get lost at times; our sight is blurred.
We are not as spiritually attuned as we can be.
We substitute gold and silver for you, Lord,
  only to discover they are illusions.
Only you, Lord, truly satisfy the heart. Amen.

Inspiration

Good morning, Lord.
Inspire those who create beauty for us:
    the sculptor, the writer, the composer,
    the architect, the painter, the virtuoso.
They feel a need to bring forth
    the new, and often the beautiful.
They can show us what you are like
    and render great service to us all.
Share your ideas with them.
Let them appreciate you, Lord,
    as the source of the talents they enjoy.
Grant courage and fulfillment to those
    blessed with singular abilities.
And for all our blessings, I thank you. Amen.

Declaring Love

Good morning, Lord.
It is important that I declare my love for you,
    to say it out loud, that I hear my own voice.
Knowing I love you without expressing it
    has far less good effect on me.
You deserve to hear the declaration.
If all of us delight in hearing we are loved,
    you too must be very pleased.
Husbands, wives, sweethearts, children
    long to hear those uplifting words:
    I love you.
You tell us of your love dramatically,
    constantly in countless ways.
It does make a difference in our lives. Amen.

September 7
Rainbows
Good morning, Lord.
Thank you for the start of this new day.
I'm pleased that the start is a grateful one.
I hate to think I am ever ungrateful.
Your blessings are here in abundance.
Positive persons can sense your gifts in life.
Flavor my day, then, with light and color.
If people say I'm naive because I see rainbows
    where they don't,
      then so be it.
Rainbows are beautiful, appearing after storms,
    golden opportunities to praise you.
Thank you for the rainbows in my life.
You express your love in many ways. Amen.

September 8
Opportunities
Good morning, Lord.
How can I please you?
Let me seek new ways to respond to your love,
    and be faithful to the old ways.
Generosity and kindness are the hallmark
    of people following your way.
Every person has so many opportunities
    to show you love
    by responding to the needs of neighbors and family.
Diligence and an honest day's work
    mean something.
Respecting your gift of life in everyone we meet
    reflects the respect we have for you.
May I—every moment—try to please you. Amen.

Highest Calling

Good morning, Lord.
Our highest calling in life is to praise you.
Whether we have attained fame or fortune,
　or are obscure ordinary folk,
　our lives have been blessed
　if they give you glory and praise.
Grace us, Lord, to be sensitive to this vocation.
Let us not be sidetracked into believing
　we can have it both ways:
　serving you and the spirit of this world.
"What does it profit a person to gain the world
　and suffers the loss of one's soul?"
There can be no compromise
　when it comes to your holy will. Amen.

Trouble

Good morning, Lord.
This is a prayer for those in trouble,
　no matter how they got there.
Trouble may spring up through no fault of our own.
It may also be of our own making:
　flirting with temptation, open to harming others.
We are all susceptible to trouble.
Help those going through it all,
　even criminals who deliberately hurt people.
Everyone has potential for good,
　and for repenting.
The worst of us can become saints.
All of us need patience, courage, and strength.
All of us need you, Lord. Amen.

Love Endures
Good morning, Lord.

In the psalms we read:

"Give thanks to the Lord for he is good:
  his love endures forever."

All our entire lives are blessings, Lord.

What other sentiment can we have
  except to tell you our gratitude?

We thank you and recognize your goodness,
  especially your everlasting love for us.

Why do you love us?

The old song expresses the mystery of your love:
  "I Can't Stop Loving You."

Inspire us to see you as you are, Lord.

We cannot help but love you more,
  respond to your love with greater intensity. Amen.

Can't Do Without
Help me not to want something so badly
  that I think I cannot live without it.

People do get into that frame of mind.

"I can't imagine not playing tennis."

Outside of you, Lord, everything's expendable.

But our attitudes do change as we mature,
  and true importance and value come into focus.

We have a passion, an obsession for things,
  such as making money.

Money is needed for pleasure, for prestige,
  for position, for making more money.

We think we can't live without something.

You're the only one, Lord, we can't do without. Amen.

Gift of Life

Good morning, Lord.
"Breathe on me breath of God,
 fill me with life anew,
 that I may love the things you love,
 and do what you would do."
I think of the biblical account of creation,
 how the spirit moved over the waters,
 how you formed man from the soil
 and breathed life into him.
Figurative language? Yes, but true.
How precious the gift of life!
Let us appreciate life, Lord, treasure your gift,
 respect it in all living creatures.
Thank you for the joy of this moment. Amen.

Nonviolence

Good morning , Lord.
Give us the grace to accept offenses patiently.
The meek, the nonviolent do inherit the land.
Our hearts go out to those who are offended
 but do not strike back in kind.
Not look for revenge,
 they are above the offense.
They seek redress of wrongs by nonviolence.
Scripture tells us, "A soft answer turns away wrath."
Bless us with this attitude.
Hatred begets hatred. Love begets love.
But hatred is dissipated in love.
Make us strong, Lord, in our determination
 to meet evil as you would. Amen.

September 15
New and Improved
Good morning, Lord.
I pray my life will be renewed and improved.
Advertisers use "new and improved"
 to say products are better than ever.
Let my life be "bettered" with generosity.
I must be convinced I can do it.
If there is hope, my renewal has begun.
Your grace is all I need for this, Lord.
Nothing is impossible, with you at my side.
Anger is overcome with patience.
Selfishness fades by caring.
Infidelity is replaced with fidelity.
I feel better knowing it is you I follow.
The new day is brighter because of you, Lord. Amen.

September 16
Your Will
Good morning, Lord.
Your judgment is better than mine
 so I pray to know your will.
It's a struggle to say "Thy will be done"
 and truly mean it in my heart.
If I could know what you know,
 all my wishes would be to please you alone.
Favor me with enlightenment and inspiration.
Reassure me and give me a child's confidence
 who walks hand in hand with a loving father.
Your saints learned this lesson
 and endured hardships for your name's sake.
"Foolish" in the eyes of the worldly,
 they drew strength from you. Amen.

Caring

Good morning, Lord.
Help me to really care about others.
"Care" is used a lot: advertisers, shopkeepers.
We hope it's not merely a come-on.
Loneliness has more to do with people not caring
    than with just being alone.
The effort to be caring has to be heartfelt.
Caring is shown in giving rather than receiving,
    in forgetting self and reaching out to others,
    in being personal in an impersonal world,
    in seeing you in the poor and lonely,
    in not counting the cost of loving.
We need to remember when we care for another
    we care for you, Lord. Amen.

Kingdom

Good morning, Lord.
In all that I do today, I want to place you first.
You and your kingdom are "number one."
We read, "Seek first the kingdom of God,"
    and "I am the Lord, your God;
    don't have strange gods ahead of me."
Sounds simple, but it doesn't always happen.
Unselfish people show us how to do it.
Their generosity and sacrifice are inspiring
    and they make your reign their priority, Lord.
Instead of asking "What's in it for me?"
    they ask, "What's in it for you?"
Thank you for this new day.
May I use it to seek your kingdom. Amen.

September 19
Daily Communication
Good morning, Lord.
Should I live a thousand years,
I wouldn't outgrow the necessity
    of communicating with you each day.
There's always a need for me to pray.
Ours is an ongoing, unending relationship
    of Creator and creature, parent and child,
    lover and beloved, forgiver and forgiven,
    benefactor and blessed.
Enspirit me, Lord, to turn to you in prayer,
    at least for a moment each day.
You tell us: Ask and you shall receive, seek
    and you shall find, knock and it shall be opened.
This is your invitation and my assurance. Amen.

September 20
Staying Human
Good morning, Lord.
Has our rapidly developing, technical,
    computerized world made us less human?
So many things have to be done right away
    and we are pressured to act like machines.
How can we make a dollar today
    and remain human, loving, rational?
It's important not to forget
    what we learned at Sunday school,
    what the Sermon on the Mount tells us:
    "Don't worry about what you are to eat,
    nor about your body, what you are to wear;
    God knows you have need of these things."
Help us, Lord, to work hard and stay human. Amen.

Being Pleasant

Good morning, Lord.
Help me to be pleasant when I don't feel like it.
Nobody loves a grouch.
At times I don't feel like joking or kidding,
    and small talk seems silly banter.
I meet people and I'd rather not
    say good morning and smile.
At the end of the day when I'm tired,
    it's especially difficult.
But the other fellow may be worse off,
    just waiting for a cue to be friendly.
We exchange a couple of nice thoughts
    and the whole day is turned around—
    for both of us. Right, Lord? Amen.

God in Others

Good morning, Lord.
Teach me to recognize your presence
    in each person I meet,
    especially the poor and the marginalized.
All creation reflects your goodness, Lord.
Each person is made after your image and likeness.
It's easy to be familiar with the famous and wealthy.
But if a person is poor or disfigured,
    that's another matter.
If someone is burdened with sadness, disease,
    that's something else.
Help me to treat everyone even-handedly,
    fairly, lovingly, generously, graciously.
It is you, Lord, that we honor. Amen.

Outstretched Arms

Good morning, Lord.
You are so patient with me.
You could punish me immediately
    for my sins, but you do not.
You have time and you wait.
You send your love and attempt
    to melt my cold, indifferent heart.
How dare I make you wait for my repentance.
Who am I to stand defiant?
But when my stubbornness of spirit dissipates,
    your prodigal child returns
    and you are there with arms outstretched.
Becoming a loving person takes some doing.
Lord, reach out and touch me. Amen.

Creativity

Good morning, Lord.
Creative people worry about running out of ideas.
Their fears are groundless if they trust in you.
We draw from your limitless creativity.
There are highs and lows in being innovative,
    times of greater and lesser sensitivity.
When we are weary and life is burdensome,
    it's harder to come up with
    winning, novel suggestions.
But that's when we ask you to refresh us.
We need to put the heavy load down
    and rest a while.
The human spirit has great recuperative powers.
Our life is from you, Lord, and in you. Amen.

Practical Love

Good morning, Lord.
"Do not be conquered by evil,
    but conquer evil with good."
If there ever was a challenge, this is it.
How to be loving when the other person
    is hateful and unkind?
I'm to respond to love by loving;
    I am touched when friends are kind.
But I'm to be forgiving and patient
    when they treat me badly and ignore me.
It means being thoroughly loving
    even in the face of rejection and injury.
Actually, there's no other way to go,
        is there, Lord? Amen.

True Love

Good morning, Lord.
I love you. I know it's what you want to hear.
We all like to hear those words
    and want them to be true, above all.
To hear them and then learn they are empty
    is devastating.
The declaration of love carries responsibilities.
"If you love me, keep my commandments!"
Loving means trying to please the other,
        doing everything possible to make them happy,
        being in harmony, willing to sacrifice,
        placing the other ahead of ourselves.
You deserve our love, Lord,
        for you have loved us first. Amen.

Cry of Joy

Good morning, Lord.
Augustine, the sinner who became a saint,
   turned his life around completely.
He speaks with deep joy of his conversion.
We are, he says, to lift our voices
   of joyous praise
   when one sinner returns to you.
He bids us "Sing to God with songs of joy."
Our hearts are to rejoice beyond words.
How pleasing it must be to you
   that we pray to you filled with delight
   that you are our God.
We know you and we are glad.
"My heart rejoices in God, my savior."
Your love, Lord, brings us peace. Amen.

Retired People

Good morning, Lord.
Many retired people don't know
   what to do with themselves.
Puttering around, they make insignificant things
   seem important.
They worked long years for this time
   and deserve this new, extended leisure time.
Inspire them with a sense of purpose.
The sick and the poor need their services.
Slow learners need their tutoring.
The sorrowful and doubtful need their counsel.
Let them not die in the spirit
   because they think no one cares.
You care, Lord. Amen.

Giving Thanks

Good morning, Lord.
How shall I give thanks
   for all the good you have done for me?
What gesture can I make
   to express my love and appreciation?
There is no adequate return I can make.
Never can I thank you sufficiently.
May I lead a good life to show my gratitude.
May all I do give honor and glory to you.
Your holy will is my constant intention.
Let me be a part of your love, Lord,
   in limitless kindness to those around me.
Let me seek better ways
   to be thoughtful and kind. Amen.

Open-Minded

Good morning, Lord.
The human mind, like a parachute,
   only works when it is open.
Truth flourishes where it is welcome.
It finds a home when we are receptive,
   willing to recognize it, even in strange forms.
Help us to be open-minded.
Each person has something to share;
   each country has something to contribute;
   each culture has values to share with us.
We need to look beyond ourselves,
   because tunnel vision is stifling.
Help us, Lord, to open our minds and imaginations
   and become creative for your kingdom. Amen.

Easy Pray

Good morning, Lord.
How easy it is to pray!
I'm so accustomed to speaking with you.
Many good people find it difficult, I know.
They have not yet arrived at easy dialogue—
    a comfortable, familial exchange.
Perhaps stern attitudes and habits of prayer
    were instilled when they were children.
Perhaps they attended church services
    where prayer resembled stuffy speech-making.
Too bad, Lord,
    because you delight in simplicity
    and in honest conversation.
Thank for this gift of communication. Amen.

Quiet Time

Good morning, Lord.
It is quiet now.
I'm getting so that I cherish quiet moments:
    time to listen, time to talk with you.
I may not have another quiet period
    until the end of the day.
As I dash from task to task,
    let me be mindful of your presence.
Speak to me, Lord.
How may I please you?
Guide my thinking; inspire my judgments.
Be with me today.
Your presence is my strength.
Thank you for this opportunity to pray. Amen.

October 3
True Friend
Good morning, Lord.
I have a true friend in you.
If I feel lonely, that no one really cares,
    I can turn to you and realize you care.
This is faith's blessing;
    believing in you makes my life worthwhile.
It has purpose and meaning because of you.
Grace those who do not know you,
    who can't find deep peace
    in the awareness of your abiding presence.
May their minds and hearts be open
    so that you may gently lead them home.
Faith is a gift of a friend
    and the friend is you, my loving Lord. Amen.

October 4
Good Samaritan
Good morning, Lord.
The Good Samaritan stopped to help
    a victim of violent mugging.
Others saw the man in need but passed by—
    helping him was inconvenient.
Help us all to be so loving and concerned
    that we never pass by someone in need.
Starving Africans are helpless by the side of the road.
Refugees from Central America knock at our door.
The homeless roam our streets.
The numbers of the needy are staggering.
If we share a cup of water
    with just one brother or sister this day,
    you will smile and bless us. Amen.

Single-Minded

Good morning, Lord.
I really understand that this is your world,
    that you have given me this day to live.
Praise and glory are yours.
Guide me. Direct me. Inspire me.
Let nothing but your holy will be my desire.
I pray for an open mind and an open heart.
This is my single-minded love:
    my human heart wishing nothing but good.
As the day wears on,
    my intentions will wear thin.
Entanglements and peer pressure
    will bring my selfishness to the surface.
Strengthen my resolve to love you in deed. Amen.

Comfortable With God

Good morning, Lord.
I ought not feel comfortable with you.
You are, after all, majesty and creativity,
    the giver of life and love itself,
    beauty, goodness, and truth.
I worship you, praise you, and glorify you.
But how disappointed you must be
    if I do not love you and consider you
    my friend, my parent, my companion.
You have called me to intimacy with you.
Being awestruck in your magnificent presence
    does not seem at all out of place.
Still, as a child I run with eagerness
    into your welcoming arms. Amen.

October 7

Our Friendship

Good morning, Lord.
How blessed I am with peaceful moments.
There are hills and valleys in my life,
    good times and bad, sunshine and clouds.
All the while I have a relationship with you.
You are my friend
    to whom I can turn in anxiety and trouble.
In poverty and pain,
    you are with me, Lord.
In times of abundance and in times of scarcity,
    you share my life.
You are my rock of security and my salvation.
Because of my faith,
    you are real, and our friendship is real. Amen.

October 8

Little Things

Good morning, Lord.
I'm thankful for the little things this day.
Someone tends to details and makes life easier:
    sugar's in the sugar bowl, groceries are on the shelf,
    directions are cheerfully given,
    people phone when they're going to be late.
Someone contributes to soup kitchens,
    checks the oil and washes the windshield,
    smiles when it's hard to be cheerful,
    and offers water to a laborer.
Someone helps with homework,
    praises a plumber's job,
    and says "I love you."
Help me, Lord, to be a doer of little things. Amen.

Childlike

Good morning, Lord.
Inspire me with a childlike spirit.
A child is trusting and candid.
There is no pretense, no arrogance.
A child is free-spirited, honest,
    and sees life simply.
A child is loving and responds to love,
    has no artificiality or sophistication,
    and is eager for love.
"Unless you become like little children,
    you shall not enter the kingdom of heaven."
Bless all our children, Lord.
They see you, Lord, and relate to you.
Help us grown-ups to be young at heart. Amen.

Dying Today

Good morning, Lord.
Will I die today?
Early Christians thought of it as "passing through."
Many people don't want to think about it.
They see cemeteries or funeral processions
    and the inevitability just doesn't register.
Help us to be confident in you, Lord,
    positive in our outlook—and realistic.
Let me live life to its full,
    singing, loving, praying, studying,
    grieving, working, crying, eating.
I don't know when you'll call me;
    it will probably be a typical day
    when I'll "pass through" to you. Amen.

October 11
Forgiveness

Good morning, Lord.
I am always in need of forgiveness,
    a necessary ingredient in life.
Everyone needs to be forgiven,
    since we are all human and fallible.
Forgiveness is a new start, a fresh beginning.
Expressing regret, being truly contrite,
    is a sincere plea for mercy and compassion.
However terrible the sin,
    the sinner finds hope and strength in pardon
    and is awakened to the reality of your love.
"Forgive us our trespasses . . ."
I ask for your forgiveness, Lord,
    to be renewed in your love. Amen.

October 12
Faith

Good morning, Lord.
This is going to be a great day!
I renew my faith in you.
There is nothing we cannot do together.
I pray to share my optimism with others.
People need cheering up;
    their confidence may require recharging.
They may have forgotten how good you are,
    how loving, how caring.
Faith makes a difference
    when they live it out on Wall Street,
    in government, offices, schools, and homes.
Faith in you will light up their day.
Bless the faint in faith. Amen.

Reflections

Good morning, Lord.
After rain storms, puddles reflect sunrises,
    or mountains, or rainbows, or blossoms.
Faith-alert people see you, Lord,
    in countless ways.
You are near—all around us.
Men and women with hearts of faith
    have no difficulty discovering you.
They see your hand
    in acts of loving kindness, in thoughtful words.
You impose yourself on no one,
    but wait to be discovered.
You reach out to everyone.
Open my eyes to see you around me. Amen.

God's Word

Good morning, Lord.
Your word is alive, full of energy.
It can penetrate deeper than a two-edged sword.
You command and it is done.
"Let there be light and there is light."
Those who hear it are moved.
Your word has power.
Men and women discover the Bible each day.
How many Bibles gather dust
    until one day, with an open mind, a receptive heart,
    they turn the pages and read it
    and their lives are transformed?
How beautiful, how compelling is your word.
Happy are all who hear it, Lord. Amen.

October 15
God's Will

Good morning, Lord.
What a blessing and grace to realize
    that nothing is more pleasing to you
    than to be intent on your holy will.
My grand plans and sincere ambitions
    must always give way to your wishes.
You know what I do not know.
For me to tell you what is best
    is presumptuous, to say the least.
I can propose; I can work hard;
I can be diligent in noble causes,
    but they must always be conditioned,
"Thy will be done."
My peace, Lord, is in trusting you. Amen.

October 16
Confidence

Good morning, Lord.
This is a new day, a fresh start on life.
Fill my mind and heart with confidence.
Let me look forward to the day's challenges,
    knowing of your care and concern,
    realizing your power and your providence,
    sensing you are at my side.
There is nothing to fear with you at my side.
Ask, you tell me, and you shall receive.
Knock on doors and they shall open.
Seek answers and you shall find them.
I cannot be afraid when you sustain me.
I anticipate your grace and strength.
Thank you for this day and all it promises. Amen.

Teachers

Good morning, Lord.
Bless all our teachers this day,
    the men and women to whom
    we entrust our most precious possessions:
    our children.
May they have the highest ideals,
    the most noble intentions,
    high academic qualifications,
    and the most effective teaching methods.
But endow them with true human values.
After us and with us, the parents,
    they mold the characters of our children.
Give them patience and understanding,
    and reward them for their noble efforts. Amen.

Repentance

Good morning, Lord.
Some people's hearts are heavy with guilt.
Free them! Let them walk with a joyful spirit.
Let them discover the key to forgiveness:
    There has to be honesty, then acknowledgment.
We sinners have to face up interiorly.
Alcoholics never get a grip on their alcoholism
    unless they admit they are alcoholics.
It works the same way with conscience.
We need not tell the world we sinned,
    but we have to recognize our sinfulness
    and there has to be genuine contrition.
I am sorry because I have offended you, Lord,
    who are deserving of all my love. Amen.

October 19
Being Grateful
Good morning, Lord.
Help me to be grateful in life,
    acknowledging my indebtedness to others.
Let no one who performs good deeds go unnoticed.
Sometimes generosity is unheralded;
    men and women go out of their way for another
    and do not receive the recognition they should.
It takes conscious effort to express gratitude.
If someone has been kind to me in some way
I must acknowledge their word or deed
    even with only the slightest gesture.
Let this entire day be one of prayerful thanks
    as I enjoy your blessings and bounty
    and the favors of others. Amen.

October 20
Seeking God
Good morning, Lord.
"When you seek me with your whole heart,
    you will find me," you tell us.
We are told that we are to love you,
    with our whole heart, whole mind, and entire being.
But to find you, to embrace you,
    our search has to be in deadly earnest.
Help us this day to be in total pursuit,
    to make you and your holy will our priority.
What does it matter if we gain the whole world—
    fame, fortune, material treasures—
    if we lose our souls in the process?
Inspire us to see your blessings and favor
    and to know that you are the source of them. Amen.

Vine and Branches

Good morning, Lord.
You are the vine and we are the branches.
Branches are alive as long as they are attached;
    cut away, they die.
To be alive, well, and thriving,
    we must be united to you.
Our relationship has to be grace-ful;
    it must be sinless and loving.
As we go through this day,
    keep us mindful of our oneness with you.
May the image of the branch
    inspire me to greater efforts in your service.
Bless me in all my efforts.
Thank you for the blessings of this day. Amen.

Beautiful World

Good morning, Lord.
This is a beautiful world:
    light snow on evergreen,
    autumn leaves in a riot of color,
    golden sun on the desert floor.
So much to appreciate, to absorb.
I really have to notice Earth's blessings.
Some men and women are so intent—
    commuting, talking, playing,
    striving for quotas, meeting deadlines—
    they never notice the beauty around them.
Their lifestyle is a drag on the spirit.
We acknowledge your beautiful world, Lord.
Bless us all this beautiful day. Amen.

October 23
Being Kind
Good morning, Lord.
Help me to go out of my way today
    to be kind to someone I don't like.
"If I am kind only to those who are kind to me,
    am I to be praised for that?"
Even the pagans act that way.
It presupposes a believer has higher motivation.
There must be people who don't like me.
Maybe they make an extra effort
    to be kind to me and hide their feelings.
Wouldn't it be great to start a chain reaction
    and have people being graci us all the time?
It would be like Christmas year 'round.
Like peace, Lord, let it begin with me. Amen.

October 24
Alone
Good morning, Lord.
There are times when I feel absolutely empty,
    lonely, alone in a sea of faces.
Other people say this, too.
I think it's important for people
    not to feel sorry for themselves.
When we begin to be too introspective,
    it's time to reach out, reverse the momentum.
There are too many good deeds to be done
    for anyone to pout and cry in their beer.
And you are willing to help, aren't you, Lord?
Your constant presence buoys my spirit.
You sustain me during the dark nights of the soul.
In that darkness, let me think of others. Amen.

Encouraging Words

Good morning, Lord.
"Have a nice day" is a positive slogan,
    an effort to be cheerful, to wish someone well.
There are other sayings I can use:
    "Good luck." "Keep your chin up!"
A plain "thank you" goes a long way.
"You're doing a good job."
"I applaud your effort." "Great game today!"
Young people need praise for good school work.
"Well done, good and faithful servant.
You have been trustworthy in small matters,
    so I am putting you in charge of greater things."
Keep us alert, Lord, to the many occasions,
    when "little things do mean a lot." Amen.

Goals

Good morning, Lord.
Help me to set goals for myself.
My life needs direction like a ship needs a rudder.
We all need purpose, a clear destination.
If I have good goals, I'll keep you in mind.
I live and work for you, not just for myself.
Shall I visit the sick, the imprisoned, the poor?
Is there a child that needs tutoring, affection, a friend?
What I do for others, I do for you, Lord.
Perhaps a goal is praying every day,
    spending a few minutes exclusively with you.
If I have not gone to church on Sunday,
    that's a goal to keep my life on course.
Good goals make me think of you, Lord. Amen.

October 27
Positive Impact
Good morning, Lord.
Occasionally a beautiful person enters my world,
    and this person lights up my life.
When a special person, a true friend.
    helps me to see the goodness in my life,
    life again becomes worth living.
All of us have the potential
    to have a positive impact on another.
We don't always recognize this influence.
Should we not try to be special to others?
A little love goes a long way.
Should we not attempt to make
    each person we meet feel special?
Will we not be imitating you, Lord? Amen.

October 28
Stir the Stagnant
Good morning, Lord.
Growth and maturity.
Is there ever a time when these reach a level?
Physically a person constantly changes.
There is satisfaction in personal development.
Help us all to strive for goals,
    never to be content with the way things are.
Give us the heart to attempt new ventures.
Stir the stagnant. Encourage the faint of heart.
Spark the dull in spirit. Quicken the sluggish.
Let us believe in ourselves
    and believe that it can be done.
You have made us creative, Lord.
Inspire us to reach for the stars. Amen.

Prayer Time

Good morning, Lord.
Is it time to pray again,
    to raise my thoughts and heart to you?
The beginning and end of the day
    are appropriate to acknowledge your presence.
There are no restrictions talking with you,
    no formality, no appointments.
How blessed are those
    who have this relationship with you,
    stopping by at any hour of the day or night.
They know they're always welcome.
This habit of regular prayer is a good one.
Sometimes it isn't even necessary to say a lot.
Lord, just see the sincerity of my life. Amen.

Divine Signs

Good morning, Lord.
Not everyone can see frost on a window.
People in the tropics may never see snow.
There is a pristine beauty in frosty designs.
With the morning sun behind a window pane,
    the frosty lines string out in unique patterns.
Why is moisture caught in such a design?
I see your hand here, Lord,
    leading us from creation to Creator.
Help me to read other signs too.
You communicate yourself constantly.
Let me know you are near
    by the smiles and greetings I encounter,
    by the beauty of your Earth. Amen.

October 31

Gravestones

Good morning, Lord.
I'd work better if I weren't so rushed.
I understand the scramble to meet schedules.
Help us to escape unnecessary stress.
There has to be time out, for you, Lord.
I might walk through a cemetery
   reading the gravestones now and then.
It's peaceful, and it puts things into perspective.
Were the people of the 1700s so uptight?
Bits of history are chiseled into these stones.
One lesson is that each day is yours, Lord;
   another is the difference between
   important and unimportant.
Thank you for the peace of this day. Amen.

Depression

Good morning, Lord.
When I feel very low and upset,
    I have to talk to you.
Even if our talk doesn't offer any cure
    for my miserable mood,
    just talking to you makes me feel better.
Since everything has its purpose,
    I hope this mood does too.
I offer it all to you, Lord.
May it be in some way for your honor and glory.
Help everyone this day
    who may be down in the dumps.
Sometimes there are no ways around obstacles,
    but only through them. Amen.

Bottom Line

Good morning, Lord.
What in the world is accomplished?
Getting something done? Attaining goals?
Each day I set out in some direction,
    things to do that day, a full agenda.
But what I did yesterday is soon forgotten,
    and only one thing really matters:
    pleasing you.
If you are pleased and honored,
    that's all that matters.
It's my bottom line.
"I was hungry and you gave me to eat . . ."
When, Lord?
"Whenever you did it to one of these . . ." Amen.

November 3
The Sick

Good morning, Lord.
There are so many in hospitals
  hoping to be made whole:
  broken bones, damaged hearts, infected lungs,
  broken hearts, and troubled minds.
When patients pray to get better,
  hear their pleas and give them courage.
Let them know of your own special concern.
Those who suffer may forget,
  that despite sickness and disease,
  you have not ceased to love them.
Give them the wisdom to say "Thy will be done."
Inspire them to see that their misery
  can be turned into your honor and glory. Amen.

November 4
Working Hard

Good morning, Lord.
No doubt we do our best work
  when we're relaxed.
Tension diminishes our ability
  to think clearly, to work reliably.
Grace those who depend too much
  on their own strength.
I think of the serious laborer, the workaholic,
  those who strain so much
  that they lose perspective of life's purpose.
Help them toward a happy medium, a balance.
In all things let them trust you.
Strengthen the sincere of heart not to lose courage.
Give them peace and refreshing rest. Amen.

Voting

Good morning, Lord.
It is a wonderful privilege to be able to choose
    those who lead us, all elected to office:
    presidents, governors, mayors, senators.
There are times when taxes rise,
    when potholes aren't filled,
    when a civil servant is found to be dishonest.
But in this land of the free—
    so different from countries
    where the people have no voice—
    we participate in fashioning our society.
Inspire us, Lord, to be responsible in our vote,
    to exercise sound judgment for the good of all.
Thank you, Lord, for our freedom. Amen.

Voters

Good morning, Lord.
For all of us voters,
    we pray that we may choose people and policies
    conductive to genuine human progress.
It is a challenge, Lord, to pay attention
    to the rhetoric and positions of candidates.
Assist us in becoming active in political life.
Policies we permit are actually policies we choose;
    not to study the issues is to vote blindly.
Not to vote at all is a failure
    to play our part in the continuing challenge
    to improve our neighborhood and world.
Motivate us to be responsible citizens,
    and thank you, Lord, for our great nation. Amen.

November 7

Stewardship

Good morning, Lord.
Come, abide in my mind and heart.
Tell me how I may please you.
I set aside my own thoughts and plans
    and seek your will this day.
What must I do to organize my life,
    to get things in order for better stewardship?
Let my priority be to honor you
    and to serve those in need.
I realize, of course, my best laid plans
    are useless unless they have your blessing.
Help me, Lord, always to be flexible
    in my pursuit of your wishes.
Not my will, but let yours be done. Amen.

November 8

Children

Good morning, Lord.
Children are the light of our lives.
Older people brighten up
    when grandchildren fly into their arms.
A home's treasure lies in the boys and girls
    who laugh and play and sing and speak.
We see beauty and honesty in children,
    a genuine simplicity that endears them to us.
They have such an ability to love,
    and to bring out love in us.
They bring us life and joy.
Help us always to welcome the little ones,
    and to treasure their childlike qualities
    which you want in all of us. Amen.

Solutions
Good morning, Lord.
When it seems there's no way out,
　　no solution to a personal problem in sight,
　　it's time for complete trust in you.
Actually, there may be a solution;
　　it may just appear hopeless.
Quandaries, problems are really opportunities
　　that may lead to you.
Many problems are solvable,
　　but we may need to call on another's help.
We need a positive, "can do" outlook.
For those who wring their hands
　　and begin to sink in anxiety, it is time to look up,
　　and see you, loving Lord. Amen.

Profitable Day
Good morning, Lord.
Let this be a profitable day—
　　not in terms of money,
　　but in terms of doing good for others.
If I can help just one human being today,
　　how worthwhile the day would be.
I can spend this day in feverish activity,
　　but it can be all be fruitless toil
　　if my only thought is of myself.
A cup of water given with a good heart
　　has merit in your eyes, Lord—
　　and helps another person.
My life is not a treadmill leading nowhere,
　　but to you, my destiny. Amen.

November 11
New Ideas
Good morning, Lord.
So often I just keep doing and doing
    without pausing to think of better ways.
Routine is valuable, patterns are practical,
    and production is often repetitious.
But some fresh thought may eliminate
    energy and expense.
Help me not to neglect the creative power
    you share with me: imagination.
It doesn't do away with hard work,
    but it can still can bring about improvement.
I've got to be open to new ideas and other ways.
Inspire me, Lord, to seek better ways to serve you.
Let it all be for your honor and glory. Amen.

November 12
Kingdom of God
Good morning, Lord.
I welcome this quiet moment.
I need it as much as food and drink.
Speaking with you at the start of a new day
    sets the tone, gives me direction.
I feel more focused with my thoughts in place.
Despite the day's challenges, I am confident
    because I walk with you.
If you are pleased with this day,
    all is well.
Help me keep this simple goal in mind:
    your pleasure, Lord,
    whatever measures up to your holy will.
Let us seek first the kingdom of God. Amen.

No Hiding

Good morning, Lord.
Help me never to be afraid of the truth;
    it's supposed to make me free.
I don't have to go about
    announcing my mistakes or character flaws.
It means I have to be honest with myself
    and face up to reality, within and without.
Deceiving myself, suppressing guilt,
    toying with my conscience leads nowhere.
Confessing—especially to myself—
    is good for my soul.
There's no hiding from you, Lord.
How immature to think you do not see.
Bless all who struggle to be open with you. Amen.

Golden Rule

Good morning, Lord.
Are you pleased with the world today?
If there is a simple guide for us,
    it must be "the golden rule."
If enough of your children do your will,
    you must smile and be pleased.
If we ignore your commandments
    and are unkind, dishonest, negligent, care-less,
    you have to be displeased.
This surely is a simple rule of life,
    but is there any other way:
    to do to others
    as we would want them to do to us?
May we respond generously to your love. Amen.

November 15
No Special Effects
Good morning, Lord.
Some say you tell them to do certain things.
I never hear voices or see writing on the wall.
That has never happened to me.
When I pray, I open my heart to you.
You listen and answer—
    in your own way, in your own time,
    with no particular special effects going on.
Believers know your will comes first, Lord.
And it is made known in the commandments,
    through my experience and rightful authority.
I guess those who declare "The Lord told me"
    are probably expressing a similar experience
    in a more dramatic way. Amen.

November 16
Small Acts
Good morning, Lord.
One kind deed is my goal today.
Resolutions to do heroic things
    generally go unfulfilled.
Just one act of kindness will change me,
    make a improvement in this world.
May all my activities this day—phoning a friend,
    writing a relative, visiting the sick,
    running an errand, serving in a nursing home—
    be acts of loving concern for others
    that will make me the person I'm called to be.
This would be a miserable world
    without these countless small acts of love.
Thank you, Lord, for the grace to do them. Amen.

Right With God

Good morning, Lord.
If everything is all right with you,
    everything is all right, period.
There is in the long run
    no workable plan without you.
Each day men and women pause and pray,
    intent to discern your holy will.
Whatever you say, it is for the best.
How silly to think for a moment
    that we can displease you with impunity.
There is peace in the hearts of men and women
    wherever your name is honored,
        wherever the sincere of heart think first of you.
Praise and honor, Lord. Amen.

Loving God

Good morning, Lord.
Loving you for yourself
    puts everything else in true perspective.
If I seek first the kingdom of God,
    details sort themselves out accordingly.
Even if I have often repeated it and read it,
    your greatest commandment still remains
    like a souvenir on a mantelpiece,
    unless I take it to heart and practice it,
    making it the dominant influence in my life:
    loving you with all my whole heart, mind, will.
I need to ask myself each day
    if what I do is pleasing to you, Lord.
If it passes this test, I'm on target. Amen.

November 19
Comfort and Refuge
Good morning, Lord.
Life is full of surprises.
No one ever has a perfect handle on life.
Just when we think everything is under control,
 running smoothly, well ordered, bingo!
If it isn't an earthquake, a death,
 a family disaster, it's something else.
Business reversals, accidents, sickness,
 emotional upheavals disrupt the routine.
For those who love you, Lord,
 everything works together for good.
Difficulties lead us to seek you in prayer.
In our bewilderment, we turn to you, Lord,
 our sure comfort and refuge. Amen.

November 20
Good Judgment
Good morning, Lord.
What makes a good judgment?
Everyday the average person makes hundreds of
 choices.
Some pan out; others backfire.
But I can't lead a productive life
 when I'm paralyzed by indecision.
Enlighten me, guide me, encourage me.
Share your wisdom and discernment with me.
Help me to see that judgments are correct
 when they lead me closer to you,
 when they help me be what you call me to be.
Still, I can't always be really sure;
 infallibility belongs to you, Lord.
Recharge me daily with your grace. Amen.

Eternity

Good morning, Lord.
At times many of us lose sight of our destiny;
     so intent are we on the short-range goals of life
     that we forget about eternity.
We grasp at straws, pursue pleasures,
     and idolize gold, silver, and power.
We think little about the treasures beyond.
Politicians preach to us about the better life
     we are to enjoy here and now.
But there is no true perspective, Lord,
     without including our eternal home with you.
Remind us, Lord, of the purpose of life:
     knowing, loving, serving you—
     and living eternally in your presence. Amen.

Kind Words

Good morning, Lord.
Let me speak words of kindness today,
     gentle words, up-building and positive words.
Fill my vocabulary with words
     that cheer saddened hearts,
     that lift up the downtrodden and disabled.
My speech is a potent force for doing good,
     golden opportunities when I meet friends,
     encounter neighbors and strangers.
Even in unpleasant confrontations
     let there be honesty, kindness, and restraint.
Let my love find expression
     in the countless words I exchange today.
Thank you, Lord, for the gift of speech. Amen.

November 23

Dying

Good morning, Lord.
Many are afraid of death.
Nothing is more final, more inevitable.
We leave the known—
    even with its trials and sorrows—
    for the unknown.
But at death, our life is not really over;
    it is only changed.
Eye has not seen what blessings
    are in store for those who love you.
If I were you, Lord, and you were me,
    I would not want you to be afraid.
Your love and mercy exceed my imagination.
Help me to trust you to bring us to new life. Amen.

November 24

Fresh Opportunity

Good morning, Lord.
Thank you for another day to serve you.
Serving those close to us is the same as serving you.
You accept the cup of water to a thirsty man,
    the food to a needy woman,
    the clothing and shelter to the homeless
    as given to yourself.
Help us to recognize you, Lord,
    in every person we meet,
    no matter their race or sexual orientation,
    their social standing or religion.
Each of us can bless one another in your name.
Let no one say they are bored
    when there is so much loving to do. Amen.

Basic Goodness

Good morning, Lord.

There is goodness in every heart.

What criminal does not have a spark
of compassion beneath the surface?

Help us to bring out the best in one another.

We need to see the potential.

As a wood carver sees a beautiful sculpture
in an ugly, snarled stump,
you see the love sinners are capable of.

If you were to judge our wrongdoing
without compassion and second chances,
where would we be, Lord?

Give us insight into the basic goodness
of the people around us. Amen.

Love With a Memory

Good morning, Lord.

Giving thanks is the right thing to do—
anytime.

Thanksgiving is like love with a memory.

People react positively when they are loved.

They instinctively want to love in return.

What better way to turn the world around
from bitterness and strife
than by showing thanks with our loving deeds?

Remembering how gracious you are, Lord,
prompts us to change our lives
and return love for love.

We need to go forth each day
and do the same with all we meet. Amen.

November 27

Evil

Good morning, Lord.
People blame you at times
    for the tragic moments in their lives.
Why did God allow this to happen?
A crippling accident, a terminal illness,
    a savage, unexplained experience.
How can an all-loving God permit this?
I must remind myself, Lord,
    that for those who love you,
    all things work out for the good—
    eventually.
We can only place our hand in yours
    and trust you completely.
I love you, Lord, in good times and bad. Amen.

November 28

New Earth

Good morning, Lord.
May I never run out of castles to conquer.
Goals inspire me.
There will never be a scarcity of challenges.
Spark my interest; fire my imagination.
Let not the sun go down
    on my desire to help someone
    or to try to make this a better world.
Let me not settle into complacency
    or think things are fine the way they are.
Renew the face of Earth, Lord,
    or better, renew my heart
    so that I may work with you
    to build a new Earth. Amen.

Other Cheek

Good morning, Lord.
"Love your enemies.
Pray for those who persecute you."
These are really hard words
      that challenge me to rise above my feelings.
I expect such big-heartedness from you, Lord,
      but from myself?
Would I turn the world around
      if I made an honest effort today
      to forgive and love those who hurt me?
Would it make a difference
      if I turned the other cheek?
If I live up to your expectations, it matters.
And it may even make a difference. Amen.

Concrete Love

Good morning, Lord.
Life is worth living when we know someone cares.
Let not my day pass without a real effort
      to touch someone lovingly.
I have to start the day alert for opportunities
      to make your love real and concrete
      through my love for others.
Let my good intentions not be a vague
      "If I can, I'll be kind today."
"Think love" is a good motto to have in mind.
Being specific slants our thoughts, words, and actions.
What can I do right here at home,
      in the neighborhood, at work, at school?
Let my acts of love be your love, Lord. Amen.

Bad Times

Good morning, Lord.
Thank you for my pain and suffering,
  my distress and difficulties.
This is not a sadist declaration,
  but an offering of my life,
  an effort to praise you in bad times.
It is a recognition of your goodness
  even in these unlikely circumstances.
It's easy to be grateful when all is well,
  but my trust and appreciation are called for
  when I don't feel blessed, but helpless.
Your mercy reaches beyond appearances.
Help me to see your goodness in bad times
  and to love you even more because of it. Amen.

Honest With Myself

Good morning, Lord.
Am I thoroughly honest with myself?
In the quiet of the morning,
  speak to me in the recesses of my heart.
Enlighten me to see myself more as you do.
Whether I reflect on it or not,
  I am always in your presence.
My secret thoughts are no secret to you.
Am I doing my level best to be a good person?
Interested in my neighbor?
Civicly responsible to my fellow citizens?
Caring and responsive to my family?
It's good, liberating to face the truth.
Bless everyone attempting to please you. Amen.

December 3

Appreciation

Good morning, Lord.
Help me to grow in heartfelt appreciation.
There is so much to be thankful for;
    I am filled with satisfaction.
I can breathe and speak; I can see and hear.
There is food on my table, a roof over my head,
    and wonderful friends to associate with.
I'm employed and enjoy good health.
I am free to worship you,
    to express myself openly,
    to travel where I wish,
    and to pursue the goals I want.
It is really a beautiful morning, Lord.
And my spirit sings out in gratitude. Amen.

December 4

Confidence

Good morning, Lord.
If there is anything I need to start a day,
    it is confidence.
I take certain things for granted;
    not that I deserve them,
    but it's good to know that they are there.
Looking on the bright side, being optimistic,
    I expect good things to happen.
My confidence is well-placed
    if it is placed in you, Lord.
I know you are listening, you care about me.
Together we shall confront the day's challenges.
Stay by me, Lord.
It's a comfort to know you are at my side. Amen.

Health Care

Good morning, Lord.

There's always a need to pray for the sick.

Who really escapes physical injury,
  emotional and spiritual illness?

We experience these in the world at large,
  in those we know and in ourselves.

Hospitals, clinics, and convalescent centers
  will never cease to exist
  for victims of street violence, wars, and accidents,
  with diseases such as cancer, AIDS, and cirrhosis.

Heal these people, Lord;
  comfort them in body and spirit.

And bless the work of those in health care.

May they carry on your mission of healing. Amen.

Answered Prayer

Good morning, Lord.

Why do you take so long to answer my prayer?

When I pray for some intention,
  it can seem like I never prayed to you at all.

How foolish—and arrogant—to think
  I can program you to respond on my schedule
  and according to my wishes.

Deep down, I know that you do answer, Lord,
  in the best possible way, in the best possible time.

I have to accept that on faith,
  and realize that I may not recognize your response.

You know what is truly good for me and others.

I'll do the asking,
  but I'll leave the responding up to you. Amen.

December 7

Creativity

Good morning, Lord.
Many people strive to be creative.
They want to do something or produce
    something useful, something beautiful.
Their creation will distinguish them.
Creativity, though, is not the property only of artists.
Mechanics, teachers, parents, politicians,
    inventors, sales people, and scientists
    also reflect your gift of imagination.
You have made us all creative, like yourself.
    capable of finding new and better ways
    of benefitting others,
    of hastening your reign of love in the world.
May we all use your gift and appreciate it. Amen.

December 8

Judge Not

Good morning, Lord.
We never really know what is happening
    inside a person.
Why are they keyed up? What's bothering them?
Do they have secret fears and inhibitions,
    with backgrounds we know nothing about?
Help me to be kind in thought, slow to judge.
    always giving someone the benefit of the doubt.
Doesn't the golden rule apply to judging?
As non-judgmental and patient
    as I expect others to be with me,
    so should I be with them.
Thank you, Lord, for helping me think of this.
You put up with a lot of my nonsense. Amen.

Nature

Good morning, Lord.
I hear the wind again this morning,
    a mournful cry, and I reject it.
I refuse to start the day on a negative note.
My imagination is not going to run wild,
    conjuring up fears about upcoming events.
Nothing will happen without your knowledge.
From the beginning of time, Lord,
    you have communicated your love.
No reason to doubt now.
Let the wind, then, sound your praises.
Let it remind me of your power and presence.
Let it remind me of your life-giving love.
I can know you, Lord, in nature. Amen.

Faith

Good morning, Lord.
Life is full of meaning to the person of faith.
You are not only the source all that exists
    and center of all life.
    but the reason for my existence, personally.
In the morning, I greet you in faith;
    during the day, we converse;
    in good times and bad, I call upon you.
In faith, I offer you each day—
    all I do and say and think—
    to praise your name.
You have blessed me with the gift of faith.
No matter what happens, it sustains me.
Thank you, Lord, for this priceless gift. Amen.

December 11
Prayer Time

Good morning, Lord.
This is when the mind is uncluttered:
    the start of a new day, prayer time,
    you and I in quiet conversation.
It's one of the best times, not absorbed in details.
You make me feel good, confident,
    because I'm aware of your personal attention.
How good it is simply to praise you,
    to tell you my inmost feelings and thoughts.
It is a feeling of interior contentment,
    just knowing—as best I can—who you are
    and who I am.
Whether folks would rate this day a success or not,
    we'll be one in mind and heart. Amen.

December 12
Blind Faith

Good morning, Lord.
I can believe you,
    even though I don't understand
    the how or why of what you do or ask of me.
Your ways are not our ways,
    but I believe in you.
I believe you are kind, merciful, and just.
I believe you created me and love me.
Now the hard part: I also believe
    that this doesn't contradict
    earthquakes, twisters, and traumas.
Your love and these disasters: how to reconcile them?
I don't; I can't, Lord.
I praise you, leaving it all in your hands. Amen.

World Problems

Good morning, Lord.

It is impossible to solve all the world's problems.

As long as we are free, as long as we remain human,
  there will be sin, trials, and problems.

Often we bring these on ourselves,
  but that doesn't mean we shouldn't try.

The world is better because
  people work hard to make it so.

It won't become a perfect place
  until we all love one another.

What a job that will be;
  it's hard even to imagine it happening.

But we have to go on trying, day in and day out,
  lighting candles instead of cursing darkness. Amen.

Sustained

Good morning, Lord.

I recognize you on awakening.

I see your footprints all around me.

From you all creation has its existence.

Overnight you sustained the stars and planets.

Earth orbited further around the sun.

You made the rain fall and the fog settle in.

Hothouse flowers blossomed to glorify you.

My every breath depended on your staying hand.

How empty life must be for the unbelievers.

I see your handiwork on the maple tree
  in surrounding hills and lumbering streams,
  in the silence of a sleeping street.

For all this, thank you, Lord. Amen.

December 15
Growing Older
Good morning, Lord.
Does it get easier to relate to you
    as I grow older?
Ours should be a developing relationship;
    we should be growing together more and more.
Our love should deepen, strengthen
    as the years go on.
How mature have I become?
"When I was a child, I thought like a child,
    played like a child, acted like a child."
For some there was a beautiful childlike rapport.
Let not the coming years, Lord—such as I have—
    bring estrangement, a drifting away from you
    through my lethargy or lack of faith. Amen.

December 16
Monotony
Good morning, Lord.
Help me to be patient in routine matters.
I do so many things over and over again,
    and there's no thrill to this monotony.
Even though I'm creative and inquisitive,
    some boring repetition is inescapable:
    the commute to work, zillions of dishes washed,
    food shopping, checkbook balanced,
    sheets laundered, reports completed.
Realistically I can't expect adventure, romance,
    and the extraordinary every hour of the day.
But may I experience satisfaction in knowing
    that I am doing ordinary things
    extraordinarily well. Amen.

December 17

Overwhelming

Good morning, Lord.
At times my life seems overwhelming.
Too many details, too much confusion,
    and everyone wants my attention at once.
The thought of being marooned somewhere
    with no telephones, faxes, or beepers
    seems idyllic, too good to be true.
But I guess it's not really as bad as it seems;
    life can be sorted out.
We may need a little help from our friends,
    some relaxation and diversion,
    some alone time with our own thoughts.
Everyone deserves a break from their routine.
Bless everyone, Lord, who takes life seriously. Amen.

December 18

Family

Good morning, Lord.
Bless our families.
Let there be happiness and harmony in them.
Mothers, fathers, sons and daughters,
    grandparents, and others,
    all need to feel wanted and loved.
Each personality must blend,
    the quick and the slow, the energetic and gentle.
Anger, harsh words, and violence
    have no place in the home.
All need to direct their attention to you, Lord.
Your presence must be acknowledged and respected.
May they live together as if you
    dwelled among them—which you do. Amen.

December 19
Morning Difference
Good morning, Lord.
The early sun slipping over the horizon
    puts things in a new light.
The reports we make, the stories we write
    take on a different perspective in the light of day.
Late night arguments, too,
    as when spouses tangle after a long day.
They say it's never good to go to bed angry.
Praying out loud and together is better.
Sunlight chases shadows.
Thank you, Lord, for this dawn,
    an opportunity to say "I'm sorry"
    and to sort out differences together.
Lord, may I make the most of this new day. Amen.

December 20
Undivided Attention
Good morning, Lord.
There is no better way to start the day
    than to give you undivided attention.
I love you for yourself.
If you never bless me with another gift,
    I will have been blessed beyond measure,
    far beyond what I deserve.
Often we begin the day thinking of
    what we are going to do,
    where we are going to go,
    what we expect to accomplish.
Does it matter, really, in the light of eternity?
You alone matter, Lord.
Loving you is the goal of my life. Amen.

Commandments

Good morning, Lord.
Your commandments are given out of love,
    not to curtail our freedom.
By obeying them we are freed
    to live safely in a community of love.
It is sweet, good, and saving to obey your laws.
Help all those who are angry
    because they cannot have their own way.
Inspire them to appreciate the commandments
    which teach us, or remind us of,
    what is reasonable: to worship you, Lord,
    to honor parents, to be chaste and honest,
    to respect the life and property of others.
Thank you for this guide to life. Amen.

Source of Life

Good morning, Lord.
The sound of the birds in the trees
    at the start of the day announces your presence;
    so does the plaintive cry of an infant
    and the rustle of the leaves, the bark of a dog.
These remind me that you share life with us.
You are the giver of life, life itself.
Help me to see your hand in everything that exists,
    to love you because you have shared your life,
    to appreciate, respect, and preserve life
    wherever it may be found.
Let me see that violence, hatred, selfishness, war
    are the enemies of life.
Lord, let love, let life succeed. Amen.

December 23
Meaningful Words
Good morning, Lord.
Words are just words until one day
   they may take on special meaning.
There are lines we have heard so often.
Then one day, their impact hits us:
   "Your heavenly Father knows all that you need."
Is this true? Is there really divine providence?
Can we take these sacred words seriously?
What a big difference these words would make
   in the practical events of life if we accept them.
We slow down and gain confidence;
   life is no longer a series of uninterrupted crises.
Lord, help me to take your words to heart
   and trust you to take care of me. Amen.

December 24
Restful Waters
Good morning, Lord.
"Beside restful waters God leads me."
How familiar are the words of your psalm,
   good words to think about when the pressures
   of daily life intensify.
I need to imagine that gentle stream,
   to sit by its banks, hear the rustle of the leaves,
   smell the verdant pasture.
Your words, once they are absorbed,
   really do bring peace and perspective.
The calm pace of the stream soothes our anxiety.
You settle me down, Lord, with a divine tranquility.
Grant me, Lord, the good sense to take time out
   and sit by the stream of your gentle presence. Amen.

Best Gift

Good morning, Lord.
What can I give you that you don't already have?
It sounds like buying a Christmas present
    for someone who has everything.
But I can offer you a gift you don't already have:
    dedication to serving you by serving others,
    the desire to do your will every day of my life.
And that is the meaning of love,
    the will to please another.
Each day I want to be able to say
    "This day is yours, Lord."
I want to live it for you, in good times and bad.
You have loved me first.
I want to return your gift and love you. Amen.

Laughing God

Good morning, Lord.
Do you ever laugh?
Since we humans laugh,
    you must have that ability too.
But laughing involves the incongruous,
    the silliness of non-matching ideas.
You know. Penguins looking like men in tuxedos;
    a child thinking you live in the bathroom
    because Dad pounds on the door each morning:
    "God! Are you still in there?"
I love to believe you get a kick out of us,
    that you too see the humor in our lives,
    that you appreciate
    our lighthearted moments. Amen.

December 27

Carping

Good morning, Lord.
How easy to say what others should do.
My neighbor should clean up his yard.
Politicians should limit financial contributions.
The clergy should give shorter sermons.
Often we use "they" to mean
   those who should do things differently:
   parents, teachers, drivers, coaches, police.
It provides a convenient handle
   to carp, to hang the blame on someone else.
Help me to realize we're all living
   in the same society with common problems,
   and if I want improvement, I have to offer
   more than negative criticism. Amen.

December 28

Morality

Good morning, Lord.
It's hard to know sometimes:
What makes something moral? Immoral?
People become deeply confused.
There is controversy about assisted suicide,
   about trade agreements and abortion,
   about the death penalty and truthfulness.
Are there objective norms? Is it one's conscience?
Is it subjective decision, which gives as many views
   as there are people? Majority opinion?
We turn to you, Lord, to help us determine
   the moral path, to seek guidance.
Grant us insight into how we are to love;
   anything short of that is off-target. Amen.

Sharing Blessings

Good morning, Lord.
When I hear the cold wind howling
    and I'm cozy and comfortable inside,
    let me not forget those who may not have heat,
    or who may not even have a home,
    and those who have to work or travel
    in the raw, bitter elements.
When I am surrounded with good things,
    I should be grateful for my good fortune.
But I should also question what I might do
    by myself or with others
    to help those who need it.
I also call upon you, Lord,
    to be with these people and comfort them. Amen.

Constant Thanks

Good morning, Lord.
Your sacred word tells us to
    "render constant thanks."
I should never stop thanking you.
You never cease to shower me with blessings.
You are my loving parent
    looking after your beloved child.
Your generosity is unfathomable,
    deeper than the seas.
Once I come to understand your love,
    my gratitude is instinctive,
    its expression natural and spontaneous.
Whatever else I may be, Lord,
    I am nothing if I am not grateful. Amen.

December 31

Talking to God

Good morning, Lord.
How good it is to speak with you again.
You, Lord, are my reliable companion
    every day of the year.
If I am lonely, I speak to you.
If I am weak and subject to temptation,
    I call upon you for wisdom and courage.
If I am confused and anxious,
    I turn to you for counsel.
If I just wish to praise you,
    you are there.
How strange it is at times to learn
    there are people who do not know how to pray.
What is more simple than loving and wanting
    to communicate with the one you love?
Thank you, Lord, for all our time
    spent together during the year. Amen.

Of Related Interest...

Scripture Reflections Day by Day
Rev. Joseph G. Donders
These 365 Gospel meditations are current, timely, and full of
meaning and hope.

ISBN: 0-89622-494-5, 366 pp, $9.95

Daily Readings with a Modern Mystic
Selections from the Writings of Evelyn Underhill
Delroy Oberg, editor
The page-a-day format offers readers the opportunity to savor
the fullness of each thought and phrase, and to keep this
mystic close at hand.

ISBN: 0-89622-566-6, 176 pp, $9.95

Seek Treasures in Small Fields
Everyday Holiness
Joan Puls
Readers are encouraged to tap into the "treasures" that lie
beneath the "small fields" of everyday life circumstances.

ISBN: 0-89622-509-7, 160 pp, $7.95

Available at religious bookstores or from
TWENTY-THIRD PUBLICATIONS
P.O. Box 180 • Mystic, CT 06355
1-800-321-0411